MORE PRAISE ~~FOR CAREER COMEBACK~~

"*Career Comeback* is the best guide to getting back on your feet when your job has been pulled out from under you. It is full of wisdom and practical advice."

> —Nicholas Lore, author of *The Pathfinder: How to
> Choose or Change Your Career for a Lifetime of
> Satisfaction and Success*

"*Career Comeback* goes straight to the heart of the job seeker's dilemma. Bradley Richardson has lived through and emerged from the setbacks associated with being out of work, so experienced professionals struggling with job loss will relate to his candor. Not only does the book touch on the emotional side of unemployment, but it also gives a solid, practical approach for getting back on one's feet—professionally and personally."

> —Jennifer Duncan,
> Director of Texas Exes Career Services,
> The University of Texas at Austin

"Buying this book is like making an investment in your life. Do it today."

> —Jeffrey Fox, author of *How to Become CEO*

"*Career Comeback* offers loads of practical advice for those facing the challenges of a career setback and looking for a way to get back on their feet again."

> —Laurence Boldt, author of *Zen and the Art of
> Making a Living*
> and *How to Find the Work You Love*

Also by Bradley G. Richardson

JobSmarts for TwentySomethings
Daddy Smarts
JobSmarts 50 Top Careers

Career Comeback

8 Steps to Getting

Back on Your Feet When You're Fired,

Laid Off, or Your Business Venture

Has Failed—And Finding More Job

Satisfaction Than Ever

BRADLEY G. RICHARDSON

Broadway Books
New York

PRINTED IN THE UNITED STATES OF AMERICA

The advice, thoughts, and insights found herein are those of Bradley G. Richardson as an individual and not in any other capacity.

BROADWAY BOOKS and its logo, a letter B bisected on the diagonal, are trademarks of Random House, Inc.

Broadway Books titles may be purchased for business or promotional use or for special sales. For information, please write to: Special Markets Department, 1745 Broadway, MD 6-2, New York, NY 10019 or e-mail specialmarkets@randomhouse.com.

Visit our website at www.broadwaybooks.com

Library of Congress Cataloging-in-Publication Data

Richardson, Bradley G.
Career comeback : 8 steps to getting back on your feet when you're fired, laid off, or your business venture has failed—and finding more job satisfaction than ever / Bradley G. Richardson.
        p.   cm.
Includes index.
1. Job hunting. 2. Employees—Dismissal of. 3. Career development.
I. Title.

HF5382.7.R55 2004
650.14—dc22   2003056271

First edition published 2004.

Book design by Nicola Ferguson

ISBN 0-7679-1557-7

1 3 5 7 9 10 8 6 4 2

To my true companion

Meredith Richardson

CONTENTS

Whatever you dream, or dare to dream, begin it.
—Goethe

The universe rewards action.
—Anonymous

ACKNOWLEDGMENTS

While the writing of a book is often a solitary task, there are many other people involved and touched by the process long before the book ever hits the shelves.

There are many people to thank, but at the top of the list the greatest thanks go to my wife and children whom I love so much. Meredith, my true companion, who has always supported and loved me, who showed strength (and patience) throughout my career comeback and throughout the writing of this book, thank you for sharing your life with me. And a huge thanks to my daughter, Samantha, and sons, Skylar and Tyler, who waited patiently as I toted around a computer or carried printed sheets around with me for months, and were always there with a smile and hug. (Yes, we can go get some ice cream now.)

This book (and my personal career comeback) would not have been possible without my agent, Patty Moosbrugger. I'm a big fan of the movie *Jerry Maguire*, and my relationship with Patty has many similarities. She is my "Ambassador of Kwan." She is a great supporter, advocate, coach, and partner. Thanks!

This is my fourth book, and each experience has been different. For the most part you work on it by yourself for months and then turn it in, but this time was different, thanks to my editor Kris Puopolo of Broadway Books. I hit the publishing lotto with Kris, who provided incredible direction and insight, and made writing *Career Comeback* a wonderful collaborative experience. She is not only a great editor who can cut through the clutter (believe me, you would have a twelve-pound book if it weren't for her), but she also sees the business side and is willing to look at all of the possibilities. Thank you so much. I also want to thank her assistant, Beth Haymaker, for patiently staying on top of the details and being so polite.

So many thanks go to my family, who have always been supportive and helped me reach my dreams: my mom, Judy Richardson, Jack and Jan Introligator, Paige and Tate Smith, Craig and Jimmy Introligator. Thanks to our close friends Steve and Shana Javery and Drs. Brad and Rebecca Weprin. Many thanks to my network of contacts, mentors, cohorts, and friends, who include Andrew Vitale; Michael Goldberg; Denis Simon of Challenger Gray & Christmas; Bob Gordon, the man who launched my writing career; Ginger Shelhimer of ACS, who coached me during my career comeback and has been a partner in our "Life After Layoff" events; Jodi Solomon of Solomon Speakers Bureau; and Cindy Colangelo of Coldwell Banker, who has always been a supporter and friend. I'd also like to thank Jerry Dickenson of the University of North Texas, who is a great supporter and has used *JobSmarts for TwentySomethings* as a text for his classes for years. Another enormous thank-you goes to Bette Scott, director of the University of Oklahoma Career Center, who, whether she knows it or not, has been an inspiration to me going all the way back to the beginning when I was a clueless student who needed career direction. Thanks to my friends and colleagues at the *Wall Street Journal,* including Debbie Knoll, Jim Graf, Marti Gallardo, and most of all Tony Lee, editor-in-chief of Career-Journal, who was instrumental in my own career comeback by saying, "You know, I have an idea, have you ever thought about . . ."

I'd like to thank the great folks at Jewish Family Service in Dallas, Texas, for putting the word out about my book and introducing me to job seekers from around the nation who shared their stories with me. Thanks to my extended network of friends, colleges, authors, and speakers who have been so helpful in offering direction, guidance, and contacts, and finally thank you to the many colleges and the university career center directors and activities professionals who have graciously invited me to speak on their campuses over the years.

—Bradley G. Richardson
Dallas, Texas

Introduction

I magine that you are driving home on a beautiful sunny day. You don't have a care in the world. You're familiar with the road. In fact you have driven it so many times it is as if you are on autopilot. You roll the windows down. As the wind starts to blow through your hair, you pop in one of your favorite CDs, turn up the volume, and let your mind begin to wander. "I'd like to try that new restaurant I read about" . . . "maybe we should take a cruise this summer" . . . "I need a haircut" . . . "I think the kids need—" BANG! Another car violently smashes into you. You are thrown forward with incredible force, only to be whipped backward from the impact of your head hitting the air bag. Glass shatters and hundreds of small shards fill the car, covering your hair and clothes. The car spins around, causing you to become disoriented. When it finally comes to a standstill all you notice is the smoke and the silence.

You have no clue what happened. You never saw the other vehicle. It came out of nowhere only to leave a path of destruction in its wake. You check yourself and although not seriously injured, you are confused, stunned, and shocked. As you climb from the car, your mind races as you quickly begin to assess the situation. "How bad is it?" "How will I get home?"

"Was it my fault?" "I can't afford for my insurance rates to go up." "That jerk should have been paying attention." "Was anyone else hurt?" "I'm lucky that the kids weren't in the car." "How much is this going to cost me?"

At a minimum you are facing a financial and material loss. Not to mention your lost time and your shaken mental and emotional state. One moment you are cruising along and the next your peaceful existence is suddenly shattered. Without warning your plans have changed and your future is irrevocably altered.

If you are wondering why I would start a career and self-help book by describing a car wreck, the answer is simple. That's because a career setback or knockdown is a lot like the scenario I just described. When you lose your job or suffer a business failure, regardless of the cause, it feels like a wreck that catches you off guard, violently shakes you, and leaves you disoriented, angry, hurt, and asking questions of yourself and others.

But a career setback isn't always a crash that results in losing your job. Sometimes getting knocked down professionally is like a breakdown along a busy highway at rush hour. You find yourself stalled at the side of the road, unable to go any farther or move ahead. Meanwhile traffic is passing you by and there is no tow truck in sight. Your career has become the lemon that is constantly in the shop. Frustrated, you want to abandon it but you can't.

Or maybe your career setback has you feeling lost and isolated. You set out toward a particular destination, but somewhere you missed the exit or took a wrong turn. The next thing you know, you are miles from your destination without a map and you have no idea how to get back.

So when you think about it, a career setback can be like either a car wreck or a breakdown. Except it doesn't matter if the wreck was your fault or not, or who got the ticket. It doesn't matter if you were blindsided or if you saw the other car coming but were unable to get out of the way. It doesn't matter if you looked at the map or if you forgot to check the tires and change the oil. All that matters is that you have experienced a life-changing setback, disappointment, or loss, and right now the most important thing is getting your career and life repaired, on the road, and running smoothly again.

You've chosen to read this book for a reason. Maybe you've realized that your work or life is missing something, but you don't know what it is or how to find it. Perhaps you've lost your business and are trying to get back on your feet. This might be the first time in your life that something you have tried has been unsuccessful or that you have met with failure or disappointment. Maybe you have recently been part of a downsizing, layoff, restructuring, realignment, contraction, elimination of redundancies, or reduction in force (RIF), or perhaps you were simply fired or "involuntarily separated from your paycheck" and feel powerless and out of control. Regardless of the reason, you are at this point of your life and career because something is not working (possibly you) and a change is necessary.

Employment has been in the news and on the minds of millions of people over recent months. Even if you yourself are not currently unemployed, underemployed, or living in imminent fear of getting a pink slip, there is practically zero chance that you or a family member don't know someone who has been directly impacted by a downturn in the employment picture.

Beyond Every Headline Is a Face

The headline in the *Washington Post* read "MCI WorldCom to Cut 17,000 Jobs." The article that followed reported the financial hit the company would take in the next quarter, the economic reason for the layoffs, and what the downsizing would mean to customers and to the company's future. But beyond the dry, impersonal "business" issues, the story failed to communicate the headline's additional impact:

◇ 17,000 families thrust into uncertainty
◇ 17,000 dreams crushed
◇ 17,000 men and women questioning how they will pay the rent or mortgage
◇ 17,000 families hoping their savings will sustain them until they find work again
◇ 17,000 men and women who regret not saving more for a rainy day
◇ 17,000 mothers and fathers, brothers and sisters, sons and daughters who must face their loved ones to explain that they won't be going to work again

Losing a job, being laid off, or suffering a major career setback or business failure has been described by psychologists as a life-changing event, on par with losing a loved one or going through a divorce. Once you lose your job or find yourself trapped in a dead-end career, everything can go downhill from there . . . professionally, financially, emotionally, and socially. Your family and relationships, your self-esteem, even your health can take a hit from which it can be difficult to recover.

When You Become "Someone Else"

People think that unemployment always happens to someone else, so when *you* become "someone else" it can be unsettling. These days no one is immune. The playing field is suddenly leveled. Millions of people currently feel out of control and out of options. An hourly retail worker can have the same concerns and anxieties as the six-figure executive vice president of a telecom firm. They both have conversations with their spouse about money, the future, and what they will do next. At the same time they silently wrestle with self-doubt, anxiety, fear, anger, bitterness, depression, or despair. These concerns result from their jobs . . . but impact every area of their lives. Work is so much more than what you do from nine to five.

When a person leaves his job, whether by choice or by force, he asks himself serious questions . . . What next? What do I do now? Why me? Who will want me? What did I do wrong? Where do I go from here? How will I get by? Have I peaked? Am I damaged goods? What will I do when the money runs out? Will I lose the house? What will my family and others think of me? These questions may be asked in private . . . and are often answered silently as people choose to suffer and search alone.

We tend to judge others and ourselves by what we do for a living. Of the many roles we play, we most commonly define ourselves by our occupation. "I'm an attorney." "I'm an engineer." "I'm a teacher." "I work for XYZ Company." When that identity is altered or threatened, we feel detached, lost, and in some cases less valuable. For many of us, our jobs are a source of pride, social standing, power, and relevance. So when you lose your job or your career becomes derailed, you may view it as a form of professional, social, or personal impotence. Peo-

ple are reluctant to discuss the emotional price or personal impact with anyone—including their own family. We like to give
the appearance that we are in control and successful. So when
the wheels suddenly fly off your career, which had been rolling
smoothly along, it becomes a personal little secret that nobody
discusses or acknowledges publicly.

Friends, family, clergy, career gurus and counselors, even
strangers are happy to lend an ear, share a weak smile, or offer
job leads, introductions, contacts, or help writing a résumé. In
fact anyone can teach a chimp how to write a resumé, what job
board to use, and that you shouldn't pick your nose in an interview. Information abounds on the nuts and bolts or how-to
aspects of job search or career management. The problem is
that nobody ever fully acknowledges the real toll a job loss or
career setback takes on your personal life and how it impacts
those around you.

This book is about making you and your life work again.
My goal is to help you experience a comeback, a resurgence,
and to give you the tools to get back on your feet, dust yourself
off, and find your stride again.

Career Comeback is dramatically different from anything you
have previously read on this subject. The advice and information in these pages are a departure from what you have heard
from any outplacement expert or career counselor you have
met with or at any seminar you may have attended. That is because as we progress over the pages to come, we will *bridge the
gap between the emotional and the practical* elements of picking
yourself up after you have encountered a major setback or disappointment in your career and your life.

Despite the plethora of books, tapes, and courses available,
opinions and advice tend toward two opposite extremes: clinical, mechanical, and "how to"–oriented information covering
only the practical elements, or abstract theory instructing you

to choose a career that will change the world or to simply "do what you love and the money will follow." The second sort tends to offer unrealistic profiles of people who at age forty-five discover their true calling is to dump their paying job and become an alpaca rancher or open a bed and breakfast. Both these approaches are valuable and have their place, yet a major disconnect occurs in the middle, where "real people" live.

The same holds true for many of the career coaches, counselors, and gurus out there. Don't get me wrong, there are many excellent ones, but in general there has been an incredible disconnect between job search and career experts and the people they serve. Rarely must a "job search" or career expert practice what he or she preaches and actually find a job or overcome a career challenge. They are simply out of touch. How do I know? Simply put . . . I've been one of them.

For over eight years I was recognized as one of America's top career and job search experts. I worked with countless job seekers and the companies that hired them, including organizations such as Southwest Airlines. I wrote, coached, spoke, and consulted extensively in this field, and, like many, looked at it from a clinical or mechanical perspective. Job search and career management was a process, or so I thought. Having already created a successful business, I never imagined that I would have to look for a job again.

But in 2000, I decided to try another entrepreneurial venture. When that company failed, I suffered a major career setback and was forced to become a job seeker myself. In case you think it was easy for me because I was a professional or had "special inside knowledge," forget it. Despite all of my experience and the fact that I knew better than the average person how to find a job, I still went through the same frustrations and fears that everyone does when looking to find work. I felt the same stress, worry, anxiety, nervousness, elation, vulnerability, despair, anger, and ultimately joy and satisfaction that everyone goes through when "selling" himself or herself. The teacher became the pupil again.

Over time, I went through the entire range of possible emotions, as did my family. I used every job search and recruiting trick I knew and learned many more along the way. I rediscovered the "tricks of the trade" and returned to my roots. I honed my techniques and skills to be razor sharp, but as I proceeded on my comeback, something else happened. I gained a new focus on my work and my family, and a new appreciation for the physical, emotional, psychological, and even spiritual impact that work (or lack of it) has on you and those around you.

Ultimately, my comeback was successful. Using many of the tools I will share with you in this book, I was able to get back on my feet both professionally and emotionally. Today, my personal and home life has never been better. I enjoy a successful career at the *Wall Street Journal*, and continue to work with job seekers through coaching, speaking, and seminars. But this time I keep it where "real people" live.

Career Comeback is the result of the lessons I learned during my own personal odyssey and from my years of helping thousands of job seekers and the companies that hire them.

We will start by taking a look at exactly what you should do the moment you find that your career has gone foul or that you are headed for a crash. From there, I'll give you a simple but powerful eight-step plan to help you do the following:

- ◇ **Find Solid Ground**
- ◇ **Find Out What Happened**
- ◇ **Find Out What Others Need from You**
- ◇ **Find Your Support System**
- ◇ **Find Out What Matters to You**

◇ **Find Your Next Move**
◇ **Find Your New Job**
◇ **Find Your Stride and Get Back on Track**

Want Things to Change? Buy a Ticket

One of my favorite jokes begins with a man praying to win the lottery. Every week, the man prays the same hopeful prayer, where he asks, "Please, God, let me win the lottery." Yet he never wins. One day, as the man once again prays, "Please, God, let me win the lottery," God finally answers and a booming voice from heaven says to the man, "I'll answer your prayer, but you have to meet me halfway—buy a ticket."

Let's get this straight right now. You can try to hope your way into a better future. You can change your attitude and your outlook. You can wish for a new job or pray for the phone to ring with lucrative offers, but the fact remains: if you don't get out there and make it happen, you will be just like the guy who wanted to win the lotto without buying a ticket.

As the saying goes, "It's not whether you fall down, but whether you get back up that counts." Are you in a situation where you've been knocked down and have no choice but to get up or give up? Are you ready to take control of your job and not let your job (or joblessness) take control of you? Are you ready for a new direction and strategy for moving ahead? Are you ready to stop letting others determine your future and learn how the game is really played, so you don't find yourself in this situation ever again? Are you ready to look yourself in the mirror and like who you see? Are you ready to face your friends and family with your head high and enjoy life again? If so, then this book is your lottery ticket.

When Your Back
Is Against the Wall

The Boy Scouts Have a Point: Be Prepared

Those trustworthy, loyal, helpful, friendly, courteous, kind, obedient, cheerful, thrifty, brave, clean, and reverent Boy Scouts have the right idea. Their motto is "Be prepared," and you would be wise to make it your motto too, at least where your career is concerned.

It has been said that luck is when preparedness meets opportunity. When you are prepared, you will have more choices, and more influence and control over what happens to you. You still may not be able to control certain outcomes, but by knowing what to look for you can at least be prepared when the worst does occur.

People plan for their retirement, they plan for their vacation, they plan what they will do this weekend, they even plan for their estate after they die. But the sad fact is that people simply don't adequately plan for losing their job or hitting a dead end.

If you haven't planned for a career setback, don't be embarrassed. People don't plan for it for the same reason they find the idea of a prenuptial agreement sickening. They feel as though they are admitting failure before they get started.

You anticipate success. But it is like when you board an airplane. The pilot and crew certainly don't expect to crash, but they still show you where the exits are and let you know that your seat can be used as a flotation device.

You may not have any warning before a bad situation occurs. You may be caught totally off guard or in a situation where you have to leave quickly. What is stopping you from being prepared? Is it hubris, arrogance, laziness, fear? "Oh, this can't happen to me." "I'll be safe." "I know lots of people." "Maybe things will change." And then there's the greatest lie we tell ourselves: "They need me." If you are still working, here are a few steps that you can take to prepare yourself now in the event you need to make (or are asked to make) a dash for the door.

Back Up Everything . . . I Mean Everything

If you learn one thing from this section, it is this: BACK UP EVERYTHING THAT IS IMPORTANT TO YOU! Back it up and keep a copy offsite at home, in a safe deposit box, anywhere other than your office.

In the best-case scenario you might have a few minutes to retrieve your files. But don't count on it. You may be shown the door and have your things mailed to you later. There are no second chances to come back. You won't have time to go through files, forward or retrieve e-mail, and make copies. Files may be blown away from your computer.

If it is a layoff or firing situation, a company will likely shut down your network access and change your password while you are tucked away in a conference room learning about your fate. Companies assume that you might be a little hot under the collar since you were just let go, so they are reluctant to let you back on to the network or near a computer for fear that you might want to retaliate by sabotaging equipment, files, or information. You will also likely have your e-mail cut off immediately so you don't send a flaming message to everyone in the company or to your clients.

Respect what is proprietary and confidential to the company. But otherwise make copies or backups right now of any projects, letters, referrals, numbers, figures, and statistics you might need. Copy lists or directories that you think may help you later in a job search. Copy your personnel files and performance appraisals and reviews.

In the best of times, make sure to back up things at least once a month. When things are shaky, you should back up every week.

Make a Duplicate of Your Rolodex and Contacts

Careers are made on skills and contacts. Some would argue that depending on your profession, contacts are *more* important. Having access to those names, numbers, addresses, and vital data is critical not only to business, but to finding another job.

Make it a point to make a backup of all your contacts, databases, and important lists. This includes client and contact names, addresses, e-mail addresses, and phone numbers. Keep both a hard copy and a copy on a remote server, website, or disk.

Update Your Résumé—Now

After backing up your information and contacts, this is the most important thing you can do to prepare. The last thing you want to do is to waste time trying to craft the perfect résumé when you are stressed out and under pressure and you need to get something to an employer. It's like filling up the car with gas before a trip. When you are cruising down the highway, late for a meeting, you don't want to stop at the side of the road to fill up. Get it done now and forget about it.

Establish a Generic Personal E-mail Account

This is helpful not only to send your backup files to, but to use as a main contact for employers and job leads. Start using your new address for résumés and in all of your job search correspondence. Both Hotmail and Yahoo allow you to set up free e-mail accounts that can be accessed from any Internet browser.

Try to choose an e-mail address that is close to your name. Some people try to choose a name that reflects their profession, like SuperSalesman@xyz.com or Great Designer@xyz.com. I think it is cheesy, but it is certainly better than an e-mail address that reflects your personal habits or interests like Born2rock @xyz.com, ozzierules@xyz.com, or suprdad@xyz.com

Create an Achievement File

Create a folder that includes a running list and samples of your achievements, kudos, and successes in your position. After a successful achievement, write a one- or two-paragraph synopsis of the project, as well as the specific results and what you learned or the skills you used to successfully complete it. Keep this at home.

When you need to update your résumé or make a case for yourself (internally or in a job search), your achievement file gives you accurate and specific information so you don't have to rely on your spotty memory.

Take Inventory

When the sky starts falling, you won't be in any mental condition to be reflective, so take a moment now to do a quick mental inventory of your career. Look at your recent accomplishments. What have you learned? How have you grown as a professional? What are you now qualified or equipped to do because of this experience? What is the likely next step if you were to leave? Could you easily go to a competitor? Do you want to stay in this field? What skills and experience can you transfer to other fields?

Renew Your Memberships and Subscriptions

Now might be a really good time to renew your subscriptions, association memberships, certifications, or anything that the company currently pays for that can help you professionally. This way they will remain active after you leave the company and you can still benefit.

Keep Up with Industry Contacts

These should include clients, people you have met at trade shows and through professional associations, even competitors. This doesn't have to be an in-depth contact. It can be as simple as a phone call, voice mail, or even a "Hey, how are you?" e-mail. You want your name to be fresh on their minds in case they have an opportunity that might be a good fit for you, or so that if you need a favor during your job search they don't think, "Huh. Who is that? Oh yeah, I haven't heard from him in a year." Start priming the pump a little bit, by putting the word out that you "might be in the market soon," "are ready for a change," or "see the writing on the wall." Begin to raise your antenna for new opportunities.

Line Up Your Referrals, Letters, and Recommendations

It can be tough to locate people who are willing to give you a reference if they are scrambling to find jobs themselves. After a successful project ask a coworker, boss, or client if he or she would write a quick note for you. Strike while memories and positive feelings are hot. Tuck that note away for a rainy day. If you think that is too bold, at least identify peers, managers, and clients who you would like to have vouch for you at some point in the future and ask if they might serve as references for you sometime.

Start to Get Your Support System in Place

Just as you should begin to identify your referrals and contacts, you should give some thought to who you can lean on in hard times . . . should they occur. This can extend to emotional or spiritual support, advice and counsel, or even financial support should it come to that. (For ideas on how to land financial support while you still have a job, be sure to check out "Get Cash and Credit While You Can" on page 52.) Give a heads-up to the people who can help you to bridge a gap in case you need it. Tell a few of your confidants so that it doesn't come as a complete shock.

Visit Your Doctor and Get Your Health Care Needs Taken Care of Pronto

If you were to ask several people who had been laid off or jobless for a period of time which was more important to them, salary or health insurance, you would likely have a pretty healthy debate on your hands. If you are in a shaky situation or are planning to make a move, get any medical needs, such as checkups, physicals, and prescriptions, taken care of now, while you still have health insurance and are not burdened by COBRA expenses.

Act Fast

If your company makes a layoff announcement or says that they might be cutting jobs in the future, act now. Do whatever it takes to prepare yourself, but act fast. Don't wait to see what happens, what the fallout is going to be, or if it will affect you. Do the things I've mentioned. If you survive it, great, you've prepared for nothing. But if it ever comes time for you to exit stage right, you are prepared.

A Storm on the Horizon

Have you ever been caught in a sudden rain shower or thunderstorm? If you are unprepared, you get soaked. It is as simple as that. Yet had you watched the news, read the forecast, or known what signs to look for in the sky, you would have been prepared. And while you couldn't have stopped the storm, you could have reacted accordingly.

The same is true in your career. You need to know some of the signs, a forecast so to speak, of whether a storm is about to hit your company, your industry, or you. You may not be able to stop it from happening, but if you know what to look for you can prepare so you aren't caught in a downpour.

Over the next few pages I'll help you identify the signs of a potential career setback.

Just because I'm paranoid doesn't mean that they aren't out to get me.
                                                    —*Woody Allen*

Signs That Your Career Is in Trouble . . . or That You Are About to Get the Boot

I want to be very clear about one thing. These are not absolute signs of a professional apocalypse. Don't overreact, panic, or work yourself into a frenzy thinking that evil forces are conspiring to get rid of you just because your boss's door is closed, you weren't copied on a memo, or your budgets are suddenly cut. Sometimes it is just business as usual and has nothing to do with you. As Freud once said, "Sometimes a cigar is just a cigar."

If one or two of these things occur, don't pack your bags

and head for the exits yet. Be rational and keep things in perspective. You are looking for consistent and dramatic trends.

◇ Your boss, mentor, or champion leaves or is suddenly rendered powerless.

◇ You fail to meet expectations or are a poor performer.

◇ You are on progressive discipline (verbal or written warning).

◇ You find yourself increasingly out of the loop.

◇ You are given a less desirable or lucrative territory.

◇ Your compensation structure changes dramatically.

◇ You are watched and micromanaged where you once had freedom.

◇ You are given new, unattainable goals or targets.

◇ You get a new boss who comes from the outside.

◇ You are in an underperforming unit.

◇ You are in a nonrevenue-producing or overstaffed unit.

◇ You are in a remote office.

◇ You have the least tenure or were the last one hired.

◇ You have a significant salary.

◇ You are no longer included in future plans or upcoming projects.

◇ You are passed over for a promotion.

◇ You fail to accept a position or relocation.

◇ Your opinion is now worthless.

◇ You are reassigned to a lower-profile project.

◇ You are demoted.

◇ You are given a "take it or leave it" or "no win" option.

◇ Management makes your life a living hell.

Your lives are in the hands of men who are no smarter than you or I, many of them incompetent boobs. I know this because I've worked alongside them, gone bowling with them, watched them pass me over for promotions time and time again . . . and I say, this stinks.

—*Homer Simpson, of the television show* The Simpsons

Make Yourself Bulletproof

It's only logical to think that working hard and being productive is enough to keep your job safe. It is great in theory, but the truth is, sometimes that is not enough. Or worse, it doesn't matter. The bottom line is no one is immune. It can happen at any time, regardless of your industry, job function, experience level, or competence. Still, here are a few things that you can do to improve the odds that the ax doesn't fall on you.

◇ Be visible—keep your name in front of people.
◇ Make a case for your value—know what value you offer to the organization and, more important, know what the organization values.
◇ Know how you are judged and what is valued—know and understand the criteria by which you are being judged.
◇ Document your results.
◇ Make your numbers, hit your goals, and justify your existence.
◇ Let your boss know that you want to be there. Don't let there be any question about whether you "love" your job, and don't assume that your management knows.

◇ Understand where the company is going—try to see the big picture.

◇ Be on top of your game—now is not the time to show incompetence.

◇ Be up on office politics.

◇ Pick your projects wisely.

◇ Maintain key relationships with clients. They can be great references if you ever need one, and they can even be great job leads.

◇ Develop your network beyond your department and immediate boss.

◇ Don't rely too heavily on your boss as your career savior.

◇ Stay away from "prophets of doom." Avoid negative people and negative information.

Know When to Jump Ship

Signs That Your Company or Industry Is in Trouble

As important as it is to be aware of how your individual career is going, it is equally important to be aware of whether your company or industry is in dire straits. Ask yourself the following questions and see if they apply to your field. Realize that not all of these are reason to head for the door and post your résumé. Some belt tightening may simply be necessary to increase effectiveness, profits, or productivity. It may just be "good business." A cluster of signs, though, may be an indication of danger.

◇ Are you in a volatile industry?

◇ Are there excessive layers of management?

◇ Is your company or are other companies in your field beginning to outsource your position or relocate it to other parts of the world?

◇ Are supplies and equipment in short supply or not being replaced?

◇ Has there been a senior management shake-up?

◇ Has new technology or competition hurt your business?

◇ Are new products, research and development, and new initiatives missing from the pipeline?

◇ Has there been a major client departure?

◇ Is the organization strapped for cash? Have they had trouble obtaining funding, loans, or credit?

◇ Is there talk of a merger, acquisition, or sale of the company?

◇ Have salaries or bonuses been cut, frozen, or eliminated?

◇ Are workers being furloughed or forced to take unpaid vacations?

◇ Have there been key staff or leadership changes or defections?

◇ Has trade show traffic decreased?

◇ Have benefits and perks been eliminated or reduced?

◇ Is there a hiring freeze or are staffing requests being pulled?

◇ Are core expenses being cut to the bone?

◇ Have they missed payroll?

◇ Does the company significantly fail to pay creditors?

◇ What is being said on the message boards and newsgroups?

Should I Stay or Should I Go?

Should I stay or should I go now?
If I go there will be trouble. An' if I stay it will be double.
—*The Clash*

The toughest thing can be to test the waters and then have the courage to jump. It can be a case of "the devil you know is better than the devil you don't." The choice to look for greener pastures or remain in your current job depends upon your individual situation, including your finances, tolerance for risk, existing opportunities, attitude, and family life, as well as the economy. Here are a few things to ask yourself that can help you to make your choice.

- ◇ Is your job making you toxic at home?
- ◇ Are you loafing on the job?
- ◇ Is now the right time in your life?
- ◇ Is the setback you are facing temporary or permanent?
- ◇ Are these legitimate concerns, or are you making too much of them?
- ◇ How long would it take for you to prepare for a departure?
- ◇ Do you need to reach a certain milestone, achieve a certain position, obtain a certain salary increase, or develop a certain skill level before you make a move?
- ◇ Have you been promised anything that may change your situation, and does your management usually keep promises?

◇ If things were to change tomorrow, would it make a difference?

◇ Can the company or job meet your needs?

Take this job and shove it. I ain't working here no more.
—*Johnny Paycheck, country & western singer*

Know Exactly Why You Are Leaving

Ask yourself if you know exactly what is the core reason that you want to leave. Is it for money, more opportunity, to escape a toxic environment, because you don't want to go down with the ship, you're bored, you want to grow professionally, to improve the quality of your life, or to escape internal politics? It may be a combination of things, but before you commit to making a move, know in your heart why you believe you are making this move. If you take a step without having this resolved internally, you will have a difficult time communicating it to a potential employer.

Put Your Toe in the Water

Go on an interview or two. Submit your résumé. Talk to a recruiter in your field. It isn't like you are making a huge commitment or getting married. You can always say no. No one will twist your arm and make you take a job unless you want to. Having a happy life and successful career is all about having options. Give yourself as many as possible.

When You've Made Up Your Mind

◇ **Don't tip your hand.** Keep your mouth shut and don't announce your plans to anyone.

◇ **Establish a time frame for action.** Create several deadlines for yourself that lead up to your departure. For example: have your résumé completed—one week; complete your research—two weeks; begin contacting employers—three weeks; have a new job—three months.

◇ **Continue to do a good job.** When a person's performance suddenly slips dramatically or it appears they have given up, it is a sign that they have already checked out.

◇ **Don't continue to wallow in negativity or self-pity and don't bad-mouth the group.** You have made up your mind. Feel good about your decision and wait until the appropriate time. You can't change things, and you know that this career is not part of your future, so don't waste time and energy dwelling on the negative aspects of it any longer.

All right, now that I've unintentionally scared each of you into looking over your shoulder and wondering when the ax will fall on your neck if it hasn't already, you are probably wondering what to do when everything does come unraveled. Up to this point you are still in the driver's seat to some degree. You can choose to stick it out, look for other opportunities, or prepare for the impending storm. In any case, the key thing to remember is to prepare. Be ready for anything and leave yourself options.

But what happens when your options have been diminished and you are dealt a hand that has left you without a job? Many of us are reluctant to make a move until we are forced to, and then it is not on our own terms. What do you do then? That is what we will discover on our comeback.

Before we go much further, I want you to understand that this is going to be a difficult journey. For some of you it may be a short one and for others it will take much longer. Each of you will approach your comeback differently depending on your resources, your background, and your particular stage in life. But it will challenge everybody. As you go through these steps, take the pieces that apply to you and use them as you would a tool. Some things are meant to be acted on immediately, and others are intended to raise issues and open your eyes to thinking about your career in a way that you haven't in the past. In the end, you control your comeback and decide where the journey will take you. Our comeback officially begins now, as we take the first of eight steps to get you and your life working again.

CAREER COMEBACK FUNDAMENTALS
When Your Back Is Against the Wall

◇ Be prepared. Always have a backup copy of your contacts and kudos, and samples of your work. Keep it offsite, away from the office.

◇ Stay in touch with your industry contacts and begin to put out "feelers" that you may be looking to make a career change or that you will soon be on the job market.

◇ Don't rely on your boss or anyone else to "look out for you" or "take care of you" in the event of a layoff or corporate downsizing. No one will look out for you like you will.

Find Solid Ground

If you are going through hell, keep going.
—Winston Churchill

In the blink of an eye it happens. Your job, your source of income, your livelihood, your community, your identity, your stability—one day it is all there and the next day it is gone. It can happen suddenly without warning, or it can be like the dull aching pain and sick relief that comes after a loved one's inevitable passing from a lengthy illness. You have lost something important. The world as you know it has suddenly changed and you have to pick up the pieces.

When you are cut (no pun intended), you need a Band-Aid to stop the bleeding. You also need immediate "first aid" when you lose your job. The first step on your comeback is to deal with the event of losing your job, determine your immediate priorities, establish a safety net, and assess and contain the financial, mental, and emotional damage.

Believe It or Not, You Can Make It Worse

Don't Blow It All by Blowing Up

You have just been handed a box and told that you have thirty minutes to gather your things. "I'll need your key and your garage pass. Good luck." Your emotions range from pain, shock, sadness, and disappointment to full-on anger or rage. As badly as you want to throw a filing cabinet through a window, tell people off, and scorch the earth on your way out . . . DON'T. In the heat of the moment you might say a lot of stupid things—things you don't mean or can't back up. It's not uncommon to become totally irrational, fueled by rage, adrenaline, and emotion. In extreme cases, people cry, yell, scream, give other people the finger, wish them a lifetime of failure, or threaten to sue. You may feel a certain bravado knowing that since you have lost your job, there isn't much more they can do to you.

> @#&⁺ you! . . . and the horse you rode in on. —*Anonymous*

It is okay to be upset. What is not okay is to become violent, intimidating, or threatening. With workplace violence on the rise, and after high-profile events worldwide where current or former disgruntled employees have entered a workplace to act upon threats, employers take this very seriously.

Even the most rational and calm person can become enraged and act totally out of character. If you threaten violence or act violently, you have suddenly escalated a highly charged situation and will likely be escorted from the building, watched carefully, and branded a lunatic . . . and that is the best-case scenario. If you are about to explode, count to three, leave the room immediately, run to the restroom and shout, leave the building—just get to another place away from people or an environment where you can harm yourself and others.

Most industries and professions are horribly incestuous, small, networked, and interwoven communities. If you remain in the same industry for a number of years, there is a good chance that you will see the same people year after year. You may even work together again at different companies. This can be a good thing or it can blow up in your face.

If you make a total jerk of yourself, burn every bridge, and generally scorch the earth as you leave, realize that there is a chance your reputation will not only be tarnished but could suffer irreparable harm as your actions follow you throughout

Do you have a right to legal action? Unless your termination has to do with discrimination or harassment or is related to gender, age, race, disability, religion, or another protected category, odds are that you might not have much to go on. Please consult with an attorney if you feel strongly that you have legitimately been wronged. But you don't have grounds to sue just because you are mad, don't like the way that you were treated, feel that it was a political decision, or simply got your feelings hurt. In most states, particularly those that are considered "employment at will" (meaning that unless you have an employment contract an employer can terminate you at any point, or "at will"), you can be let go for almost any reason, as long as it is not discriminatory. Think long and hard before pursuing legal action. Your best bet may be just to get on with your life.

the remainder of your career. People talk, people move around, and yes, people remember.

> I'll get you, Dorothy . . . and your little dog too.
> —*The Wicked Witch of the West, from* The Wizard of Oz

"Here Is a Check . . . and There Is the Door"

> Go on, take the money and run.
> —*The Steve Miller Band*

When the big day arrives and you are called into a conference room with your boss and a person from human resources, they may explain that it is not a personal decision but things are tough, or that things aren't working out and changes have to be made. The HR person then goes over the details of your departure, including severance, if you get it.

There are no guarantees regarding severance. An employer is not required to give you a severance or termination package—unless you fall under a union agreement or have an employment contract that outlines what the termination policy is. Not everyone receives it and you aren't entitled to it. There are no laws that dictate you must receive two weeks' salary or compensation when you are fired or leave an organization.

How Are Severance Packages Determined?

While there are no hard-and-fast rules, the general rule of thumb is that the average worker receives two weeks' compensation for every year of service. That can vary wildly from company to company. It can also include pay for any unused vacation, sick time, or floater or comp time. Some companies even choose to limit the maximum amount of severance that a person can receive. (Not a popular move for people with a lengthy tenure.)

Severance payments can be made weekly, according to your current pay schedule, or as a lump sum. It is up to the employer. In addition, severance payments are taxed as regular income, so your severance package may be $4,000, but your check won't net you that much.

Unfortunately, as many people discover the hard way, the best time to negotiate a severance agreement is when you are hired, and not as you are being shown the door. Don't worry. I'll give you tips for doing that later as part of Step 7 (Find Your New Job).

What Might a Package Include?

Most severance packages are determined by position, length of service, or salary and compensation level. They can include cash, but often will include additional training or career services (often called career transition, career management, or outplacement services) to help you in your next job search.

Why Do Employers Offer Severance Packages?

It is essentially a goodwill gesture to help ease your transition and cover your expenses until you find your next job. Not wanting to be seen as a completely cruel and heartless organization, they are offering you something to take the sting out and help you bridge the gap. While it can't prevent you from pursuing legal action, it is intended to subtly sway you from it. It is both a public relations move and a financial move.

But I Was Promised . . .

You may have been made certain promises that your boss would look out for you, help you, provide you with something, or protect your job. Maybe he said that you were safe. Great. Do you have proof of this? Do you have it in writing? Sorry. There are a handful of limited situations where a verbal promise is binding in an employment situation, but unfortunately verbal promises are pretty much worthless or unenforceable. Get everything in writing and run it by a lawyer.

Everything Is Negotiable . . . I Mean Everything

One of the laws I live by that has served me well over the years is simply this: "If you don't ask, you don't get." Sometimes the answer is still "no," but unless you ask, it will always be "no."

Few times is this more important than when you are leaving a company. You are stunned, scared, and certainly miffed, but don't let those feelings or a momentary lack of composure keep you from getting all that you deserve and cutting the best deal for yourself.

Yes, I said cutting a deal. Too many people make the mistake of accepting a severance or termination package as if they are being served a bad vegetable in the school cafeteria line. It stinks, but you let the lady with the hair net put it on your tray anyway, without saying a word. You have let the organization spank you once by taking your job; don't let them do it again by giving you a bare-bones cookie-cutter package and sending you on your way.

First of all, ask for a detailed explanation of all that is included in the package. You want to know the amount of the payout and the terms. How will it be paid? When will it be paid? If training, outplacement, or transition services are being offered, ask for specifics. Who will be providing it? How long will the services be for? What specific services are being offered? Are you required to use their provider or do you get a choice? What if you don't need to or choose to use the transition services they offer? What are the details about continued health coverage? What about any stock options you have?

The person conducting the meeting may or may not have all of the details and answers you need. Don't let them push you out the door and run over you. And whatever you do, don't let them pressure or intimidate you into signing anything unless you are completely informed and comfortable.

Be Creative

What is most important to you? Don't automatically say money. Of course money is important to you . . . but let's take a look at some other things that you may miss when they are gone. How about office space, your company car, your cell phone, pager, BlackBerry, or PDA? What about your e-mail, Internet access, or your laptop? It can be a variety of things that have value. Sure, you could probably pay for many of those things on your own with the severance you are going to receive, but why not ask? Convenience has a price too and besides, you need to focus on your comeback, not on shopping for the best cell phone plan.

Get creative. You can certainly start by asking for more money. There is no harm in that at all. Of course, be reasonable and realistic in your expectations. Unless you are a pretty high-level senior exec, or had previously agreed to a set amount, you're looking at anywhere from two weeks to a best-case scenario of around three months.

Remember that your severance is often taxed, and generally commissions or bonuses are not automatically factored into severance. If you were going to receive an annual bonus, you might ask for a prorated amount.

Other things that you might ask for include continued use of your cell phone, e-mail, or Internet access. You might negotiate continued use of your laptop or even ask if you can purchase your laptop, PDA, or other equipment from the company. If you have a company car, negotiate continued use until you can purchase, rent, or lease another one. Ask if you can lease it back from the company in the interim or purchase it outright.

I've known people to negotiate continued use of their office space and equipment as they conduct their job search. They would show up every day just as they did when they were full-time employees, except now they would conduct a job search. One guy in particular negotiated space for two months after his position had been eliminated.

You might consider negotiating for cash in lieu of the services that you don't need, don't want, or would like to pursue on your own. This might include training, transition, or outplacement. These can be incredibly valuable services, so I strongly suggest that you carefully consider taking advantage of them if your employer offers them.

However, if you are extremely confident in your job search abilities and ability to weather the storm on your own, or if you are simply at a point in your life where you will not be pursu-

Vanessa, a marketing executive at a Fortune 500 consumer goods company, was told that her small department was being disbanded and that her job was being eliminated. A sizable outplacement package was part of her severance. However, Vanessa and her husband had already decided that if something were to happen to her job, she would not continue working, but would become a full-time mom. Armed with this knowledge, Vanessa said that she did not want or need the transition package, so she was able to negotiate the cash value of the package, which was several thousand dollars that she was able to put in her pocket.

ing a transition, you might attempt to negotiate for the cash value of the services.

Okay, What Is the Catch?

Nothing is free in this world and this includes severance agreements. Each is unique. However, one of the more common elements is the "mutual release." A mutual release can be written to include a variety of things, but most often it says that in exchange for the severance package you are to receive, you and the company agree to mutually "release" each other from any future claims or damages. This is to protect your employer from having you come back in the future and sue the company.

This is a serious CYA (cover your ass) measure on the part of the company, and rightfully so. Losing a job can bring out the absolute worst in people. Rather than getting on with their lives, some poor souls spin their wheels by plotting how they can get back at the company. Often, filing a frivolous discrimination, harassment, or wrongful termination suit is one way of doing that. By signing the release you might agree not to sue or speak ill of the company or take any future legal action related to your employment or termination.

Should I Sign Anything?

You should not sign anything without carefully reviewing and completely understanding what it is you are signing, and then only after you have had a chance to calm down. Never sign anything in the heat of the moment or simply because they stick it in front of you. If you are threatened or intimidated, that is even more reason to take the paper home and review it.

The moment you sign something, no matter how harmless, you give up a significant amount of power. If you want to negotiate anything, do so before you sign a release. In addition, if you legitimately believe that you have been wrongfully terminated or discriminated against, then you should talk to an attorney before you sign anything.

What About Noncompetes and Nondisclosures?

Sometimes, a condition of receiving your severance package is that you sign an NDA (nondisclosure agreement) or a noncompete agreement.

An NDA (nondisclosure) is the most common agreement. It basically says that you will not divulge any company secrets or bad-mouth the company in the press or in public.

Noncompete agreements are more rare. They basically restrict you from working for a competitor, in the same industry or a similar position, or establishing a similar business for a specific period of time. The average Joe and Jane don't really need to worry about this. Noncompetes usually matter only if you are a senior executive or possess critical inside information.

Noncompetes are usually written so that they extend to a specific geographic region, a particular industry, or a period of time, and they cannot impose unreasonable demands such as preventing you from working in that field. Depending on where you live, noncompete agreements are extremely difficult for an employer to enforce. Courts tend to frown on limiting a person's ability to make a living.

Agreements of this nature may have been previously agreed to or negotiated when you were hired, possibly as conditions of an employment contract (assuming you signed one), so make sure that you review any materials you received or signed when you were hired. You can't and shouldn't ever be coerced into signing such an agreement. Don't ever let anyone pressure you to sign anything limiting your rights, especially while you are in an emotionally charged situation or if you haven't studied it. Take it with you and show it to an attorney.

This, too, is a negotiation. If an employer expects to limit you or prohibit you from doing something, then you had better get something significant in return.

Acknowledge Your Emotions

When you finally get the news that you are being let go or you realize that your career has veered completely off track, you will go through every possible emotion imaginable. You may feel shock, loss, betrayal, anger, sadness, a sense of failure, or fear. Everyone handles it differently.

Some people go into a catatonic state of disbelief where they are incapable of functioning. Some become Chicken Little and take a fatalistic view that the sky is falling all around them and there is no hope, while others go into denial by adopting a Pollyanna view. It is important to keep a positive outlook and believe that everything will be all right, but you should also be pragmatic. Blind optimism (or denial) can prevent you from taking actions or making tough decisions that may be necessary. Surprisingly you may even find that you feel some sort of relief, as if the announcement has finally put you out of your misery. Sometimes the anxiety caused by wondering if and when the ax will fall can be so stressful that when that day finally comes, you welcome it. At least now you know what is going to happen and can get on with things.

Regardless of what you are feeling, the best thing you can do is to step back for a moment and breathe, calm down, vent, yell, explode, do whatever you need to do for yourself to get your head straight, *before* you call anyone, share your news, or make a snap decision.

I Need a Job—Stat!

When you lose your job, one of the other things you lose seems to be your ability to judge and discern . . . at least for the first few days. The initial shock can quickly give way to desperation and panic. The result is a burst of energy that can ultimately be counterproductive.

It becomes easy to think, "I need a job, I need a job now . . . any job. Right now." And so you begin burning up the phones, calling your old contacts, recruiters, and search firms, grasping for straws as you work yourself into a chaotic frenzy. This is a huge mistake. Your anger and fear come across as despera-

COMEBACK EXERCISE

Believe it or not, what you are feeling right now (as much as it hurts and as sick as it makes you feel) will prove to be a valuable experience that you will want to remember. Really. Here is what you do. Write yourself a letter. Write down your concerns, worries, and exactly what you feel right now and what you felt as you were let go or shut down your operation. This is not about the gory details of what happened, but about how you feel. Read it, sign it, and date it. Stick it in an envelope and place it in a drawer. This will be important down the road, after you have found your next job and found your stride, to show you how far you have come.

tion. Slow down and get yourself together before calling anyone. Your first order of business is to tell your family and the people close to you who are directly affected by your loss.

> The best thing about the future is that it comes only one day at a time. —*Abraham Lincoln*

Everyone Goes Through This . . . or Knows Someone Who Has

When you lose a job or lose your business, it feels as though a giant spotlight is on you, pointing out to the whole world that you no longer have an income or that you have failed on some level. Even if your career setback was the result of a layoff that has affected thousands of people, you still feel as though you are the only person in the world this is happening to.

In the past, there was a stigma attached to being without a job, regardless of the cause. During the height of the dot-com craze I heard one recruiter remark, "If someone is not working, either they don't want to or there is something wrong with them."

How times change. With downsizing, layoffs, entrepreneurial failures, and a sagging global economy, losing a job (or knowing someone who has lost one) has become almost commonplace.

Many of the high-flying, headline-grabbing entrepreneurs who once inspired envy have closed shop and landed salaried jobs. They've also had to buy a tie and put the sandals away.

When a company announces layoff figures, they can number in the thousands, affecting not just individuals, but entire neighborhoods and cities. At one point last year, one Zip Code in an affluent suburb of Dallas, Texas, had the fastest-growing unemployment rate in the nation after several of the area's major telecommunications firms announced thousands of layoffs.

Many recruiters and headhunters are now unemployed themselves. According to some estimates, the recruiting and executive search industry shrank by almost 40 percent last year, and some of the most prestigious firms closed offices and reduced their staff by as much as half.

The point is . . . you are not alone. You have not been isolated or singled out. You are not the first person this has happened to, nor will you be the last. Granted, it is not a club that anyone ever hopes to join, but new members are being initiated every day.

The public's views on career setbacks and job loss have

changed, much like the public's views on divorce have changed over the years. While no one embraces it, divorce has become so common that it no longer holds the public stigma it once did. The good thing about this (if there is one) is that there is no longer any stigma, shame, or negative impression associated with a career setback except for what you impose on yourself.

Breaking the News to Your Spouse or Partner and Other People You Care About

No one ever plans for this conversation. There is absolutely no easy or comfortable way to do it, but here are a few tips to make it less painful for everyone involved.

Do It as Soon as Possible

Don't wait around for the "right time." (There is none.) Don't kid yourself by thinking, "I don't want to upset them" or "I don't want her to worry." You aren't doing anyone a favor by sparing them the truth.

Tell Them in Person, NOT on the Phone

Tell your family in person, particularly your spouse. Don't do it over the phone if at all possible. Your first reaction might be to call from your car after you leave the office. If this was shocking or upsetting to you, imagine how they will feel. Sharing news like this over the phone is bad on two levels. First, if they take it poorly, you're not there for support. Second, calling them at work or in some other public situation can prove to be a mistake because they might become overwhelmed. Wait until you both get home and break the news in person.

Don't Sugarcoat It

Be realistic about what happened. Try to be factual and avoid being dramatic. Don't try to sugarcoat the news, tone it down, or offer a diversion. They are trying to process what happened and need to come to terms with it on their own.

This Will Hit Them Personally Too

How did you respond when you were told that you had lost your job or at the moment you knew that your company was not going to make it? Shock, anger, confusion, fear? Did you react out loud, yell, or scream? Did you cry, or did you sit there in stunned silence trying to process it all? Remember that feeling, because your family will likely respond similarly when you break the news to them.

By the time that you break it to them, you may still be upset, but you will have at least been through the initial surprise or sickness. Prepare for them to go through the same thing.

You may come home and expect comfort and support, and you will likely get it, but be prepared for them to go through many of the emotions that you experienced. This will hit them as personally as it did you.

Don't Try to Fix Things Immediately

The point of this first conversation is not to solve the problem; it is to communicate the situation. They may ask, "What will we do?" or expect an instant answer. Unfortunately you don't have one. You can only reassure them. You might say, "I don't know what is next or what it will mean, but my first priority is to work it out. I know that we'll be okay."

Depending on your partner's personality, they may comfort and sympathize, or they may jump right in and try to fix the situation then and there: "Okay, here is what you need to do." That may be their style and how they believe they can help. It tends to be a typically male reaction to "fix it" right away and offer comfort by "solving the problem," but that may not be what you need. Speak up.

Before you make any major choices or begin to think about your prospects, your next move, or anything else, get your bearings and get through the initial loss first.

They Can Be More Upset Than You Are

If there was tension in your marriage or relationship before, this can send it over the edge. A job loss can exacerbate any existing tensions or frailties in a relationship. Whether it is a legitimate concern or not, a partner may blame you for not doing enough, trying hard enough, playing the game well enough, being assertive enough, taking your job seriously enough, or even for failing to see what was going on. They may wonder if there is something else behind the story, or if you were simply incompetent. It can be a greater shock if it is completely out of the blue. "How can this happen? You are such a good employee and work so hard. There must be more to it." Attempt to explain clearly what happened and why.

Even in the most solid relationship, there may be a brief moment of doubt when a spouse, parent, or partner wonders, "What did they do?"—especially if you have a history of job hopping or sketchy employment. Your partner or family may need reassurance that it wasn't your fault, and if it was that you learned from it, will correct it, will never let it happen again. Regardless of the cause, your challenge is to restore their confidence in you at a time when your confidence in yourself is shaken. It may take time.

They Don't Care What Happened to Anyone Else . . . Just You

You may have been one of thousands to receive a pink slip. Your job loss may be the result of a massive restructuring that made national headlines. Your spouse or partner really could care less. There is little comfort in the fact that others lost their jobs too. To them it is personal. All that matters is what happened to you and what it means for your family.

If You Have Kids—Show Stability

Be honest with your kids and tell them in age-appropriate terms what has happened. For younger kids you might simply say, "Daddy is going to get a new job, and he may be around home for a while until then." It may mean telling them that you aren't going to eat out as much, that they will need to take better care of their toys and clothes. Explain how they can help. They may not fully understand what this means, but they are concerned and can notice changes and sense stress.

Clearly communicate to children that any changes will be temporary. If you are married, it is best for you to tell them together with your spouse. It is important that they see stability at home. The same is true if you are a single parent. Your child needs to know that while employment situations change, your love is a constant.

Establish Your Safety Net . . . and What to Do If You Don't Have One

When You Boil It Down, It Is All About Money

Harvey MacKay, one of my favorite business authors, once wrote that "if you have money and it can solve your problem, then you really don't have a problem." He is right. I don't want to appear crass, but when you boil it down, how you approach your job loss depends largely on your financial situation. I'm not saying that it still doesn't hurt or isn't a blow to your self-esteem, but simply that your outlook, the choices you make, and the urgency with which you act are based largely on whether or not you have a financial cushion or safety net.

Having a financial safety net, in the form of savings, a working spouse, a family that can help you out, investments, or a significant severance, means that you can make different choices than you would if you had to find a job in the next couple of weeks. A safety net means that you can have more patience when weighing options or exploring your next move. It also means that you have less stress at home. If you are fortunate enough to be in a situation like this, count your blessings.

However, it is probably more likely that you are one of the millions of people who are living paycheck to paycheck or have a cushion that can only withstand a few weeks of unemployment. It is nothing to be ashamed of. It seems to be the norm in our consumer-oriented culture that worships instant gratification. It also just costs a lot to live or raise a family.

The difference is that when a person who is living check to check loses his or her job, their world can quickly become unraveled. They also lack the array of options that someone with a reserve or cushion has.

You Know That Rainy-Day Fund? Well, Get the Umbrellas

What is a safety net or cushion? Having a cushion doesn't mean that you are wealthy. It just means that you have a little bit of money put aside so that you can pay the mortgage and the bills for a few months, or at least have a place where you can turn to help you make ends meet until you land your new job. Some experts say that you should have a cushion of at least three months' salary, but let's get real here: if you are a family of four making $60,000 a year, you might not have $15,000 lying around for your rainy-day fund, so you have to look in other places.

Your safety net can take the form of a severance from your former employer, savings, investment accounts that you can liquidate (other than for retirement or education), or it can be a spouse or partner who works or a family member who can loan you money in the short term. The point is that you have somewhere you can turn to in the short term.

Whether you have a safety net or whether you have to watch every penny as if it is your last (because it is), now is the time to be mindful of your money and finances. Each of you will respond differently depending on your own financial situation. I realize that some financial experts will probably shriek in horror at some of these suggestions, but for many of you this step is about survival and landing on your feet, not financial planning.

If you are fortunate enough to have a financial planner or accountant whom you trust, by all means please consult with him or her the moment you find yourself in this situation. Don't wait. The second person you tell about your situation, after your family, is your financial advisor. A planner or accountant can be an invaluable resource and prevent you from digging yourself in a hole.

Whether you have a nice cushion or if you are living hand to mouth, here are some tips to consider when you find yourself "in between" jobs.

Cash Is King

How does your cash look? Do you have any savings, money market, or cash accounts that are liquid should you need them? Cash is king right now. Cash means that you can take care of things without accumulating debt or liquidating valuable assets such as stocks, home equity, CDs, or retirement accounts.

Apply for Unemployment Benefits ASAP!

If you don't apply for unemployment benefits, you are making a huge, costly mistake. I don't care how much you were making or what you did for a living, unemployment insurance is there for the taking. The funds have been paid into a fund by your former employer through taxes for this very reason. You are automatically entitled to them by the state.

Of course there are some restrictions, and how much and how long you receive unemployment assistance varies from state to state. However, the average is around twenty-six weeks, and payments can range from a couple of hundred to over four hundred dollars a week. Not exactly a king's ransom, but it can cover a car payment, groceries, or utilities. Contact your state's unemployment office or workforce commission for details. The United States Department of Labor has links to state agencies at www.doleta.gov.

Each state has its own unique standard, but generally the major requirements to qualify for unemployment are that:

◇ You must be unemployed through no fault of your own (meaning that you can't be fired for misconduct like theft, insubordination, chronic absences or tardiness, or have resigned). However, you can collect benefits if you were fired for poor performance or incompetence. In some cases you can also collect if you were forced to resign. If you are ever threatened with "resign or we will fire you," don't take the bait (unless you have done something grossly inappropriate). It is often easier to prove that you qualify for unemployment benefits if you are fired.

◇ You must have worked for a certain period of time for an employer who has contributed to the unemployment fund through taxes.

◇ You must be able to look for work.

A notable exception to this is that freelancers, contractors, and other self-employed workers often can't collect unemployment. Being self-employed, it is likely that you never paid into the unemployment fund. Again, check with your state office to see if you qualify.

Talk About Kicking You While You Are Down

Be careful. Your massive unemployment check will be taxed as regular income, yet the money will not be taken out of your check as it was when you were employed. This means that you will need to plan ahead so you can pay taxes on it come April. Yes, it stinks in the worst way possible. The ray of sunshine is that you might offset some of this income with expenses related to your job search, which are tax deductible. Keep your receipts so that you can claim all of your qualifying deductions.

Is Filing for Unemployment Looked Down On by Employers?

Absolutely not! This is not like a poor credit report or a criminal record. It is not a barrier to getting a future job. Unemployment benefits are not welfare, and there really is no stigma attached anymore. Much of the process can be done online or via telephone, so it is not like you are going to see anyone you know down at the unemployment office or workforce commission. You don't score points or get a badge of honor for not taking it. Swallow your pride and take the money.

What Are Your Additional Sources of Income?

Even though you lost your job, you might have additional income streams. Do you receive any dividend or other investment income, or royalty income? Do you have a rental property? If you have additional sources of income, ask yourself how much you can generate, what it can cover, how consistent or frequent it is, and how long it will last.

Get Liquid or Know How You Can Quickly

If cash flow is going to be a concern for you, then you should take a look at whether you need to sell any stocks, property, cars, boats, electronics, or anything that may tie up your cash. I'm not suggesting a fire sale. However, if you are short on cash and have money tied up in other assets, particularly noncritical or depreciating ones, you might consider converting them into cash should you need it.

Don't Think of Your Severance as a Windfall

Did you receive any severance or termination pay? Was there any type of payoff or deferred compensation? If so, how long will it last? Is it two weeks' or two months' salary? How will it be paid out? Is it being paid as one lump sum that you can budget and parcel out, or will you receive it in equal amounts according to your former pay schedule?

Don't make the mistake of thinking, "I have six weeks' severance so we are ahead right now." This may be your only income for a while, so use it wisely until you get back on your feet.

Turn a Hobby or Skill into Cash

Do you have a hobby or sideline that you can use in the short term to earn some cash? I'm not talking about pursuing a second career or starting a company, but is there anything you can do as a part-time job or home-based business? The possibilities are endless. Do you have skills that would allow you to accept freelance or contract opportunities? One attorney I

Brett had kept his condo he lived in before he got married and used it as a rental property. That rental income proved to be a life-saver when he lost his job. As his unemployment dragged on, he and his wife chose to downsize, selling their house and moving into the rental property, which by this time was paid for.

know did contract and freelance work writing wills out of his apartment after his firm downsized. A marketing and public relations executive was laid off on Friday and by Tuesday had a two-week contract writing press releases for a major event to be held in town.

You should also consider signing up with temporary agencies to get some part-time or occasional work. It can get you out of the house and generate some money as a cushion. You can always turn down the assignment that day if you have an interview. You can consider starting a basic home-based business selling cosmetics, doing yard work, or selling homemade cookies or jewelry. The point is, if you are creative and open, you can generate some income in the short term as you proceed on your comeback.

Sell Your Junk: Have a Garage Sale or Yard Sale

A new job means a fresh start. Why not freshen up your house and make some money to boot? Not only is a garage sale or yard sale a great way to clear out your garage, attic, or spare room; it is an awesome way to generate cash quickly.

Get rid of all of your old clothes, books, and CDs, and the Roy Rogers wagon-wheel coffee table that your wife hates. It adds up. It is not uncommon to make $500 to $1,000 in a weekend (depending on the quality of your junk).

You might also consider selling baseball cards, memorabilia, or other collectibles that you aren't attached to, online at eBay.

Keeping It in the Family—Family and In-Law Financing

No one wants to go back to Mommy and Daddy for help, regardless of how old you are. You think that you are a self-sufficient adult, and when you have to turn to family or in-laws for cash or financial assistance it can be a humiliating experience that makes you feel like a twelve-year-old asking for an allowance.

While few will say it, inside your head you keep hearing a voice scream "Loser!" As uncomfortable as it may be, if you are forced into this situation, you should throw your pride out the window before you make some really dumb decisions. Your family and others may be willing to help you however they can. You can make a formal loan arrangement with interest. Or it could be a zero-interest gift. Be careful. Any amount over $11,000 given in one year is subject to a gift tax. If this is the case, know that the person who is giving you the money can take a big tax hit.

Your family and closest friends love you and may help if they can, but realize that it can cause additional stress on these relationships. Beyond the obvious obligation of one day paying them back, your immediate obligation is to be extremely thankful and appreciative, and demonstrate a serious effort to becoming reemployed.

Get Cash and Credit While You Can

If you see the writing on the wall, you should apply for all loans, credit cards, or lines of credit while you can still qualify. Things to consider include:

◇ Refinancing your home
◇ Applying for a home equity loan, signature loan, or credit extension
◇ Applying for low-interest credit cards

Once you lose your job, it becomes infinitely more difficult to obtain loans or credit. You may never access the line of credit or use the extra credit cards you applied for, but they are a little insurance policy that you can tuck away for later should you ever need it.

Home Equity Loans or Lines of Credit

If you have equity in your home and need cash, you have the option of refinancing and pulling money out of your home equity or obtaining a home equity line of credit. These are not very good options, but nonetheless they are ways to get some cash if you are sinking with no prospects in sight.

While many banks and lenders market home equity loans as a great way to consolidate debt, experts say that swapping unsecured debt (credit cards) for secured debt is not a smart move. You've suddenly put your house in jeopardy. Now, that may seem extreme. I don't mean to sound like an alarmist—home equity loans are an incredibly useful tool for improvements. But I suggest that they be used as a means of last resort.

You may get a better interest rate than with other methods, but there is too much at risk.

Cash Advances on Credit Cards

As you can see, we are going in order from the most to least desirable way to create a safety net. We are now approaching the bottom of the barrel. Getting a cash advance on your credit cards is another way to grab some cash for a rainy day, but it often comes at a steep price. Most card issuers charge a transaction fee for cash advances, and they are often charged at a different, sometimes higher, interest rate that would make Tony Soprano or your average loan shark smile. You should do this only if you are really in a bind. This is the option of last resort.

If you have a card that does not charge fees for cash advances or offers an interest-free or reduced rate period for cash advances, that is not a bad deal. You could do that and then flip the charges onto another low- or no-interest card later. But, again, this is not a habit you want to get into.

Raiding the 401(k) and Retirement Accounts

Well, here we are. About as low as you can get. When all else fails, you can turn here, but I (and just about every financial planner on earth) would advise against it. While there are certain circumstances in which you are allowed to borrow from or remove money from your 401(k) or other retirement accounts without penalty (buying your first home, college education expenses, major medical expense), this should only be done as a course of last resort.

Raiding your retirement account is costly on many levels. The first is that if you take money out of your retirement account before you reach retirement age, you are not only taxed on the money, you pay a 10 percent penalty to the IRS. You could end up only getting about 60 percent of your money.

The other reason you don't want to touch it is because it would be incredibly difficult to make up for that money. The value that the account has accumulated tax-deferred over time can never be made up. Sometimes it is unavoidable, but you should consider every other option possible before doing this.

Identify Your Immediate Priorities and Expenses

A popular business axiom states, "It is not how much you make but how much you keep that matters." Well, when you aren't making anything, keeping what little you have becomes even more important. Since currently you have finite resources (savings, severance, etc.) and no income to replace what you are spending, it is critical that you not only know how much of your money is going out the door, but that you hang on to as much of it as possible.

Determine Your Monthly Overhead

What is your monthly nut? What does it cost you to live each month? One of your most important tasks in finding solid ground is to determine what your total expenses are. I mean everything—your bills, your necessities, your incidentals, your miscellaneous expenses, the entire total.

As you review your checkbook and statement, write down each expense and the dollar amount for the past month. Your list should include everything: mortgage, car payment, electric, grocery store, haircuts, and kids' lessons. Dry cleaner, cell phone, baby-sitter, car insurance. Keep track of everything. Now, more than any other time, you need to account for every dollar, drachma, and dinar that you spend.

What Quarterly or Annual Expenses Do You Have?

Make sure that you include any major or infrequent expenses too. For example, you may have homeowner's or life insurance premiums that are due annually or quarterly.

What Additional Expenses Will You Now Have to Cover?

If you are going to have to pick up additional health insurance coverage through COBRA, don't forget to write that expense down. You'll also want to include any expenses that your former employer covered, like cell phone, gas, or car, that you will now have to pick up. Last, don't forget any loans or payments that were automatically deducted from your check that you will now have to pay on your own.

Know How Long Your Money Will Last You

Any dot-com refugees and start-up junkies out there will be all too familiar with the term "burn rate." Essentially the burn rate is a calculation that shows how fast you are burning through money, and is used to determine how much time you have before you run out of money, or "burn up."

Similarly, you need to know how long you can go without an income before you run out of money. It is pretty simple to figure out. Take your total amount of cash, savings, or other resources and divide it by the total amount it costs you to live for one month (all expenses). The remaining number is how long you have before you run out of cash, assuming that you have no income at all. For example, if you have $12,000 in cash and savings but your expenses are $3,000 a month, then you can last four months. Knowing where you stand is critical not only to your finances, but to your emotional state and that of those around you.

Know Your Benefits

Have a clear idea of what benefits your employer provides and how their loss will affect your family. Do you receive benefits like a gym membership or child care reimbursement? Do you get a company car, or does the company pay for your cell phone? As you review your benefits, ask yourself if each one is something that you and your family can do without or something that will have to be replaced immediately and paid for by you until you find another job. If you will have to replace benefits, what will your costs be? Where can you turn to find those services? Who provides them? Know these things in advance so you aren't totally surprised.

Identify Any Major Upcoming Expenses

Do you have a costly auto or home repair that is unavoidable? Is there tuition due? What about property or income taxes? Are you or a family member facing any medical procedures?

Where Can You Immediately Cut?

Are there any expenses that you can cut out all together? For example, do you really need the "total platinum every-channel-known-to-man" package on your cable or satellite? Do you have any extravagant or expensive entertainment costs that you can eliminate or even recoup by selling your tickets? Do you really need to dine out every other night, or could you cook at home? Do you have a vacation planned that you can cancel or get a refund on? Do you really need your yard guy, or can you mow the lawn yourself? Get those pasty legs outside behind the mower and save yourself some money.

What Can You Put on Hold?

Which of these expenses and obligations are set in stone and which can be altered, postponed, or cancelled? Depending on your situation, you might have to consider changing your plans. Okay, you can't tell a baby to wait, but if you and your spouse were planning to try for a pregnancy soon, you might want to hold off a few more months. If you were planning to move or build a house, you might think about waiting until next year. You can't put life on hold, but you want to be smart and realistic.

Check whether you are eligible for any early payment discounts or extended monthly payment offers. Which things are absolutely essential, can't-live-without items?

How tight you make your budget depends on your financial situation and comfort level. Base it on your existing expenses and funds. It is great to be positive and think that it won't take you long to find a job, but the truth is that it will probably take you a little longer than you think. So hope for the best, but prepare for the worst.

Cut out waste and frivolous things. You don't have to go on a bread-and-water austerity budget. A common mistake is to panic and cut areas that can actually be helpful in landing another job. For example, cutting out baby-sitters and caring for the kids yourself while you are at home can save money, but then what do you do when you have an interview or need some uninterrupted time to focus on your search?

"Do I Really *Need* It?" Versus "Do I Really *Want* It?"

Until you get back on your feet, every time you are about to make a purchase ask yourself this question: "Is this a 'need to have' or a 'want to have'?" At this time, you should focus on

It is staggering what we blow money on every day. Much of it is unavoidable. You have to have a place to live and a car or at least some form of transportation, you have to pay your electric bills, and obviously you have to eat. On the other hand we are all capable of throwing away cash as if it were Monopoly money. I personally have shelled out the equivalent of a brand-new car to the good folks at Starbucks. If you want a good look at what your frivolous spending really costs you in the long run, check out David Bach's *Smart Couples Finish Rich*. He coined the phrase "Latte Factor" to describe how we throw huge sums of money away on things like . . . well, Starbucks. Good stuff. Read a chapter for free at www.finishrich.com.

what you need rather than what you want. Sounds harsh, but it will help in the long run.

You should also ask yourself if you need something "right now" or if it can wait. Delay your gratification. This can mean waiting to get a new car or a new house, or make a repair. It might even mean doing a repair yourself. You might consider taking a less extravagant vacation near home for a couple of days rather than the fancy trip for a week. It can mean eating more meals at home or staying at home a few extra times to save on sitter costs.

Decide Which Bills to Pay First

Obviously you want to pay all of your bills on time, but if you are in a crunch always pay your secured debt before you pay your unsecured debt. Secured debts are things like your mortgage or your car. Unsecured debts include your credit card bill and your gym membership. If you pay your Visa bill late you may get an annoying phone call and a negative mark on your credit record, which isn't good. But if you seriously mess up with your mortgage or your car, your lender can take it away. So pay the secured first. Better to have Visa mad at you than dodge the repo man. There are also other expenses that you can't let slide and that should take priority over unsecured debt, including your basic expenses like your utilities, rent, and phone.

If you find yourself falling behind, first contact your creditors and explain your situation. This is tough and requires you to swallow your pride. Don't sugarcoat the situation or wait until it is too late.

If you are being harassed or threatened by creditors or collectors, you should know there are laws that protect you from harassment. Contact your state attorney general's office for information.

Another great resource to turn to is consumer advocate and credit expert Benjamin Dover. He is a columnist and author who offers excellent information on how you can deal with creditors and stop the harassment. He can be found at www.bendover.com. (Stop giggling like a fourth-grader. Yes, this is his real name and it is a legitimate site.)

Contact Important Creditors While You Can

If you have a lot of debt or are starting to get behind on your bills, the smartest thing you can do is to contact your creditors, before things get ugly. Many have programs and special offers for customers who have lost their jobs or are experiencing other hardships. You would be surprised—there are special plans for everything from your car payment and mortgage to your credit cards, and creditors are usually more than willing to work with you, if you contact them at the onset of a problem and don't wait until you get really behind.

This does not mean that you are a loser or a deadbeat, and often it will not affect your credit or appear as a black mark, or at least not as negatively as if you blow off debt completely.

Plans vary but can include options such as deferred payments, meaning you are granted a couple of months' reprieve or interest-only payments in exchange for extending the term of your agreement or tacking those extra payments on to the end of the loan. Mortgage companies can extend the length of payment, allowing you to skip a payment and add it on at the back or even suspend payments until you are employed again. Credit card companies may be very willing to reduce your interest rate or allow you to pay a reduced rate or no interest for a certain period of time. These programs are usually time-based for anywhere from three to twelve months. The key to any of these programs, or "workouts," as they are commonly called, is to stay on top of your payments and stick to the agreement. If you don't, the agreement can be cancelled and then you are really up a creek. As with your family, communication is the key to working with your creditors. Also, keep copious notes. Get the name or ID number of everyone you talk to.

Think About Refinancing Your House

If you get into problems with your mortgage, you need to talk to your lender ASAP. Don't think that you can wait. You can always put Visa off for a month; you do NOT want to put your mortgage company off at all.

Foreclosures and delinquencies are up, but only a fraction of homes scheduled for foreclosure actually make it to auction. In many cases the lender and the homeowners come to new payment terms. If you have enough equity in your home, you may renegotiate the note, bringing the mortgage up to date. If things get really dark, one option may be to seriously consider downsizing temporarily and renting out your home. That way you can at least hang on to it and have the rent cover the mortgage.

Review Your Insurance Benefits

The loss of a job is scary. The loss of income can be frightening. But for many it is the loss of health benefits that keeps them up at night.

You are entitled to continue your insurance coverage under what is known as COBRA. This is great because even though you lose your job, you don't instantly lose your insurance. The catch is that it is often outrageously expensive to continue coverage. You are essentially purchasing an insurance plan through your former employer at the group rate; however, instead of your employer paying the premium (or a major part of it), you pay for the entire thing. This can easily cause your cost to triple or go even higher than that.

If your spouse works and has insurance, you should try to add yourself and your family to that policy. It will be infinitely cheaper. Most plans allow you to add additional family mem-

Even though your boss or human resources person went over your benefits package and presented a cursory overview of COBRA and other insurance options, you were most likely in a stupor. If you have questions, call your human resources department back after the dust has settled. Get them to clearly explain everything and learn whom you need to contact regarding (1) health coverage; (2) remaining expenses or monies due to you; (3) 401(k) or other company-sponsored retirement packages; and (4) stock options. Even though the ties have been cut, they will likely help you sort through these issues, although they are not legally obligated to do so.

bers or make changes to the plan (outside of the open-enrollment period) in cases of a life-changing event such as a marriage, birth, or change in a spouse's employment status. Have your spouse check with his or her human resources department for details.

It always pays to shop around. Getting insurance on your own can cost a downright fortune. But there may be other options that are more attractive than continuing through your COBRA coverage. If you belong to a professional association or trade group, they may offer group insurance rates for their members. (This is another reason to renew your memberships before you leave.) Call your association headquarters

COBRA (CONSOLIDATED OMNIBUS BUDGET RECONCILIATION ACT)

Under this act all employers in the United States with twenty or more employees must offer coverage to exiting employees. COBRA gives you the opportunity to extend your health coverage for up to eighteen months. However, the catch is that instead of your former employer paying the premiums . . . you are now paying the entire tab. You also pay a 2 percent fee to cover the employer's handling fee for processing the plan for you.

After you leave your company, you will receive a notice about your rights to continue coverage, and you have fifty days after you receive that letter to accept or reject the coverage. On average COBRA costs are estimated at around $600 per month for a family. That puts you in a tough spot if your unemployment benefits are totaling a little over $1,200 a month.

and ask if they offer group or discounted insurance plans for members.

Put Everything into Perspective

Okay, How Bad Is It Really?

No matter how brave a face you put on in front of others, internally, a job loss or career setback can rattle even the most optimistic and self-confident person.

"My life is over." "I'm a giant fraud." "I'm a failure." "I'll never work again." Sound familiar? If you aren't careful you can easily let your thoughts get out of control, shaking your confidence to the core and letting yourself become consumed by self-doubt, negativity, and completely irrational thoughts.

Irrational thoughts are false. They are the lies we tell ourselves. They are not true, they are not based on fact, and they are not productive. They also have no place in your comeback. They are like enormous potholes in the road.

Let's do a little exercise here to see how rational you are being.

Below are a few common "irrational" statements that people who have experienced a career setback may utter to themselves. I'm sure that you have your own choice ones. Feel free to add them to this list. As you read each one (including your own), ask yourself objectively, "Is this true?" "Is it based on fact?" "Is this thought productive, and will it help me to get what I want?"

- ◇ I'll never work again.
- ◇ My spouse will leave me.

◇ I'm going to lose the house and will have to live under the freeway.

◇ Everyone will think I'm a huge failure.

◇ Nobody will hire me.

◇ I'm too old/I'm too young.

◇ My parents/third-grade teacher/ex-wife were right, I am a loser.

◇ Nobody wants me.

◇ Nothing good ever happens to me.

Let's look at some of these statements rationally. Take "I'll never work again." Are you sure about that? It may be true that you will never work as a VP of business development in the telecommunications industry again. It may be true that you will never work as an e-commerce solutions consultant or a flight attendant again . . . but will you work again? Yes, if you want to.

How about "I'm going to lose the house and will have to live under the freeway." Let's see, do you have a roof over your head right now? Are you current with your rent or mortgage? Is the sheriff at the door threatening to evict you? If, God forbid, you must downsize or sell the house, could you move to a smaller house, an apartment, or a different part of town? And if that doesn't work out, as unpleasant as it may be, could you stay with your parents, in-laws, or brother until you get back on your feet? In fact, as you are sitting in bed reading this, you are actually about four or five really big steps from being homeless and living under a bridge, so drop it.

The point of this exercise is to make you realize how over-the-top, crazy, and unproductive some of your thinking can be. If it isn't helping you move forward, improve your relationships with others, or get a job . . . then you shouldn't be thinking it. You don't have time.

The world is still spinning around you, but at least you have started to gain some control and are beginning to find solid ground. The challenge now is to start moving ahead, but in order to do that, we must first determine what has just happened to you.

CAREER COMEBACK FUNDAMENTALS
Finding Solid Ground

◇ It is perfectly normal to be angry, sad, and show emotion.

◇ Break the news to those closest to you in person, not over the phone. Don't wait. Do it as soon as possible. They may be as upset as you are.

◇ Don't be forced into signing anything until you have had a chance to review it.

◇ Always try to negotiate more from a severance package. Be creative and consider extended use of equipment, offices, or other benefits. If you don't need any of the additional benefits your employer is paying for, try to negotiate the cash value.

◇ Review and establish your safety net immediately. Cash is king. Avoid debt and credit if at all possible.

◇ Identify your immediate priorities and expenses. Create a budget and know where you can cut, if necessary. Quickly determine how much money you have and how long you can remain without a job before you either run out of cash or have to dip into savings and other funds.

◇ File for unemployment benefits ASAP!

◇ Contact creditors early before there is a problem. Many have programs for this situation and will work with you.

◇ Review your insurance benefits. If your spouse or partner has benefits, have yourself added to the policy. It may be cheaper than paying any COBRA expense.

◇ Stop to breathe, calm down, and examine what happened and where you go from here. Don't freak out or go into "I need a job now!" panic mode. Put things in perspective. Read on.

Find Out What Happened

Some people make things happen. Some people watch things happen. And some people say, "Hey, what happened?"

—Anonymous

Have you ever known someone who always seems to be in a bad relationship? Such people feel incomplete and inadequate when they are without someone, so they quickly move from one relationship to another as if to avoid being caught in limbo . . . alone.

I have a friend like this. He is sharp, nice-looking, intelligent, and successful, yet he goes from one destructive relationship to another. His relationships are almost always unhealthy, and after investing months and in some cases years, he comes out hurt, disappointed, and wondering what went wrong. But rather than take the time and effort to reflect on his relationship, review the signs that should have tipped him off that things were going downhill, ask himself what was successful about the relationship, or question the type of people he is consistently attracted to, he leaps headfirst into the next relationship, never breaking the cycle of disappointment.

A career setback is a lot like any relationship that has gone bad. If you don't learn from your mistakes, then you are doomed to repeat them . . . most likely in your next job. If you aren't careful and make your next move without taking stock of what has happened, then you can easily find yourself in a pattern of disappointment or frustration.

The problem for most people after a career setback is that they are so eager to get away from a bad job or are so fearful of being without a job that they jump from one bad or incompatible situation to the next . . . just like jumping from one relationship to the next. If you have been knocked down and you don't stop to see what caused you to stumble, then you are setting yourself up to fall again. It is as simple as that.

When you lose a job or your career is suddenly derailed, everyone asks some variation of "Why?" Whether it happens quickly, without warning, or whether they watched the approaching tidal wave long before it crashed, most people find themselves stunned and asking, "What just happened?" Yet very few people actually take the time to honestly answer and explore these questions.

To Go Forward, Start by Looking Backward

I love television shows and novels about coroners and crime scene investigators. I'm fascinated by Patricia Cornwell novels, whose main character is a medical examiner, or television shows like *CSI: Crime Scene Investigation*. I'll even watch old reruns of *Quincy, M.E.* Part detective, part scientist, these investigators perform autopsies and analyze the details of a crime to determine the cause of death or nature of the crime.

Why would I mention something so . . . well . . . creepy, and what does it have to do with your career? I believe that after a career setback, one of the first orders of business is to conduct a postmortem or an investigative review of the recent developments in your career to determine what went wrong.

In one of my recent seminars I introduced the subject of conducting a postmortem on your career. Dan, a man in his late forties, loudly objected. "I totally disagree. Why in the world would I possibly need to look back? What's done is done. It is in the past so why worry about it? I'm an optimist. I only focus on the future."

Dan was pretty worked up. So I complimented him on his positive outlook and agreed that "yes, looking toward the future and not dwelling on the past is the only way to really move forward." But as we talked, I learned that he had been with three companies in the past eighteen months and couldn't understand why. By forging ahead without learning from his past experiences, Dan was setting himself up for a cycle of failure.

> We don't receive wisdom; we must discover it for ourselves after a journey that no one can take for us or spare us.
>
> —*Marcel Proust*

The next step in picking yourself up is to reflect on what has happened in your career up to this point. The following exercises will help shape your outlook, free you from beating yourself up about what has happened, and move you that much further in your comeback. Now don't worry, I'm not talking about a search for your inner child at work. I am talking about devoting a couple of hours to facing what happened and asking yourself if you are a victim of circumstances beyond your control or if there was something you had some influence on that may have caused this outcome.

This requires you to be totally and brutally honest with yourself. It asks you to revisit uncomfortable events and face your own possible shortcomings. I never said this would be easy. The good news is that this is for your eyes only. There will not be a quiz later, nor are you expected to include this on your résumé or bare your soul to your friends, family, and potential employers. No one but you will ever know, care about, or judge your answers. So don't hide, filter, or manipulate your responses. The more truthful you are with yourself and the more honestly you assess your actions and events, the more effective this exercise will be and the faster you can get back up.

The Only Real Failure Is Failing to Learn

> I've missed more than nine thousand shots in my career. I've lost almost three hundred games. Twenty-six times, I've been trusted to take the game-winning shot and missed. I've failed over and over and over again in my life. And that is why I succeed.
> —*Michael Jordan*

It is important to understand that this "postmortem" is not intended to beat you up any more than you have been, nor is it meant to be a "fishing expedition" to find fault in your career. While the magnitude of everyone's setbacks is different, it is easy to think that you have failed at some level. Even the most optimistic person has moments of doubt, second-guessing, and wondering, "If I'd only done this." "If I'd only seen the signs." "If I'd only acted sooner." "Where did I go wrong?" "Was it me?"

These feelings, no matter how temporary or unfounded, can be daunting and can drag at you like an anchor, preventing you from moving forward. Yet something can truly be considered a "failure" only if you fail to learn from the experience or fail to correct your behavior so that it does not happen again.

If you study and learn from the experience when it does occur, then a setback can be a significant step in both personal and professional development. (Although you probably won't realize it until long after you have found your stride again.)

What's to Review? Isn't It Obvious? Management Destroyed My Company

"My CEO was a crook." "My industry went down the toilet." "9/11." "My job was moved to India." "My company went out of business." You might be thinking, "Find out what happened? I already know what happened. What do I have to review? My setback was broadcast on the news and made the headlines."

There are dozens of career setbacks that are totally beyond your control. Even if your setback involves a public news event, like a mass layoff, and everyone in the country knows it is not your fault, your ego can still take a hit. Intellectually, you can know the reasons for the setback, but your emotions still cause you to ask, "Why me?" You begin to question the system and the idea of fairness. Self-doubt and second-guessing place incredible pressure on you that can keep you from moving forward.

Reflecting on what happened can help restore your self-confidence by assuring you that the problem was beyond your control (if that is what happened). Or it can give you an idea of what to look out for next time so that you aren't caught off guard and can have more control over your career in the future.

What is this place? How did I get here?
   —*The Talking Heads, "Once in a Lifetime"*

When it comes to job loss or setbacks, there are two steps in reviewing what happened. The first is to review the events, actions, and circumstances that were completely *beyond your control* or where you had no significant input. The second is to review the events, actions, and circumstances that were *under your immediate control or influence.*

Circumstances Beyond Your Control

Let's start by taking a look at items that you likely had no control over, yet that impact your position. According to DBM, the world's largest outplacement firm, 86 percent of people in their career transition program lost jobs through no fault of their own. Job losses were due to mergers, closure, or restructuring. (Of course this doesn't take into consideration the scores of displaced entrepreneurs and employees of smaller organizations and start-up companies who don't utilize outplacement firms.) When these things happen, often there is nothing you can do about it no matter how talented or tenured you are. Sometimes these decisions are made according to strict regulations, contracts, predetermined agreements, or a systematic culling of employees. It has nothing to do with your abilities, your performance, your work habits, or even your track record. It may simply be an across-the-board, every-department-has-to-cut-10-percent mandate. Selections may be according to a last-in, first-out policy whereby the most recent hire is the first one to be let go. They may be based upon a ranking system where the bottom 10 percent is asked to leave . . . regardless. It is hard to say that it isn't personal, because it affects you so personally, but in the majority of mass layoffs, and especially closures, a broad sword cuts indiscriminately.

COMEBACK EXERCISE
What Happened: Beyond My Control

The following is a list of events or circumstances that are typically beyond your control. This is by no means a comprehensive list, but as you go down it, ask yourself whether each event or circumstance occurred in your organization. You will notice that some of these items are similar to the signs listed in the opening chapter that show your company may be in trouble.

Now, take a piece of paper and at the top of a page write "What Happened: Beyond My Control." As you are reviewing the list of possible things that were out of your control, ask yourself, "Was I aware this was going on?" Did you have prior knowledge of it? Were there rumors or buzz about these things, or did you have a "gut feeling" or sense about it? If so, what tipped you off? Write down each of the following situations that you feel was applicable to your company or you.

- ◇ Was I part of a mass layoff or restructuring?
- ◇ Did my company lose or fail to receive funding?
- ◇ Was my company involved in a merger, acquisition, or buyout?
- ◇ Did my department move, restructure, relocate, or close?
- ◇ Did I have the least tenure?
- ◇ Was I in a satellite office or remote location that was closed or relocated?
- ◇ Was my job or department relocated or outsourced (perhaps to another part of the world)?
- ◇ Was my position eliminated because it was redundant or being duplicated elsewhere in the company?
- ◇ Did my company overhire?

◇ Did unethical, crooked, or poor management hurt my company?

◇ Did my company suffer from an economic or industry downturn?

◇ Was my company dependent on another industry that suffered?

◇ Did my company's stock price or market performance decline dramatically?

◇ Did my company lose a valuable client that made up a large portion of billings or revenue?

◇ Was I in a unit or department that was underperforming, non–revenue producing, or noncritical to operations?

◇ Was my department overstaffed?

◇ Was there a major management shake-up?

◇ Did I get a new boss who cleaned house?

◇ Was I a contract employee or temporary staffer?

◇ Is my industry considered volatile, turbulent, or obsolete?

◇ Did the company run out of money?

If you answered positively to any of these questions, you haven't failed. It is not your fault. You are a victim of circumstance and situation. You can't dwell on it. That may sound simple, and I know if you are like most people you will vacillate on this. Even though you can see in black and white that these reasons are legitimately beyond your control, you will backslide occasionally and wonder "Why me?" "What could I have done?" Don't. Your talents, abilities, and skills are the same now as they were when you were happily employed. Sure, there might have been signs and you might have seen the writing on the wall, as we discussed earlier. In hindsight you might notice other signs that things were going downhill. But the only thing you can do about it now is to recognize these signs in the future, use your newfound experience to react accordingly, and move on.

> **There are no mistakes, no coincidences. All events are blessings given to us to learn from.** —*Elisabeth Kübler-Ross*

It's important to understand this because when you present yourself to a potential employer, confidence is crucial. As we will discuss at length later in the book, if you appear weak, unsure, and shell-shocked to an employer, you will have an uphill battle to fight. You may not like or fully understand why this has happened to you, but if you come to grips with the fact that your current situation has nothing to do with your skills, intelligence, or work ethic—with you as a person—but was due to an external force sweeping you along, then you can present yourself confidently.

Actions and Events Under Your Control or Influence

Next we'll take a look at the actions and events that you actually controlled or had an influence over. In any job, like any relationship, there are causes and effects. Your actions and words may influence a decision or outcome that has a lasting effect on your career. Often you don't realize the cause until much later. That is what this exercise is for.

> **There are no wrong turns, only wrong thinking on the turns our life has taken.** —*Zen saying*

COMEBACK EXERCISE
What Happened: Under My Control

As you did earlier, take a piece of paper, and this time write "What Happened: Under My Control and Influence" at the top of the page. Same drill as before. Ask yourself if each item listed applies to you. As you ask yourself each question, search your memory for a specific example. If you can find one, write it down. Frankly, this list is tougher to read because the questions are personal. Do yourself a favor. Take your time with this. Don't just blow through the list and think, "Nah, this doesn't apply to me."

Did I hang on too long?

Did you overstay your welcome? Sometimes you can stay with an organization too long and overstay your usefulness. Over time, it is possible to lose your passion for what you do unless you are continuously challenged and advancing and periodically refreshed.

Was my setback a self-fulfilling prophecy?

Did you subconsciously want this to happen? Did you want to change jobs, leave the company or the industry, but didn't have the courage to move unless you had no choice? Was sabotaging yourself an easier way out because you weren't going to make a change unless forced?

Was my boss a tyrant? If so, did I try to learn how to deal with him or her?

You may think that a horrible boss is something beyond your control, but you do have some control over how you respond. Did you try to learn how to work with him and adapt to his style, or did you chalk it up to "He is a jerk"?

Did I have blind trust in others or in "management"?

Being loyal and trusting people is one thing. Accepting everything that is put before you without asking your own questions is another.

Did I understand and play the political game?

Unfortunately, if you have three people in a room, you have a political situation. It doesn't matter if you are with a large or small organization, politics exist everywhere. Did you understand how they worked at your organization, or did you think that you could avoid them by putting your head down and working hard? Everyone has to play the game to some degree.

Did I step up and accept a key project or leadership role?

Sometimes opportunity is not handed to you—you must reach out and grab it. Did you pass up an opportunity to shine waiting for someone to give you permission or a green light?

When given a leadership opportunity or a chance to shine, did I blow it or not live up to my potential? Did I make the most of opportunities I was given?

Did you have chances to excel, impress someone, or show what you can do, but you fell short? Could this failure have soured your reputation? How could you have corrected it?

Did I offend or make an enemy of the wrong person? Did I have any personality conflicts with anyone? Who? Why? Were they influential or important?

Did you step on anyone's toes inadvertently? Maybe you had a showdown with a peer who was well connected, with your boss, or with an influential person in another department.

Did people like working with me?

You don't have to be the life of the party or the most popular person in the office. You don't even have to be agreeable all the time. After all, everyone has bad days or weeks, but were you toxic to be around? Were you a complainer? A politician? A nitpicker? Did you always have to be right? Did you not let other people share opinions or get a word in? Did you hinder other people from doing their work?

Was I abrasive, pushy, or obnoxious?

Being pushy isn't always that bad, but did you cross the line to the point where people didn't want to deal with you? Having a reputation as a maverick or for being aggressive is one thing. Having a rep for being a pain in the butt is entirely another.

Was I considered a leader or a follower?

Did people follow you, look to you for answers, or use you as an example or role model, or did you blend into the woodwork, beige and nondescript? Even worse, were you used as an example of what not to do?

Did I overestimate how important or valuable I was?

C'mon, we all think that the earth will stop spinning on its axis if we leave an organization, but in truth it keeps on spinning and companies keep on running long after we have departed. Could you quantify your value to the company, and how did it stand in comparison to that of your peers? Also, was your value (at least what you consider to have been your value) something the organization really cared about? Very few people are truly irreplaceable.

Did I have tantrums or give ultimatums?

Everyone loses his or her temper once or twice, but did you go too far in threatening or overreacting? Did it become a habit? After a while it gets old and people stop wanting to deal with you.

Did I lose interest? Was I bored? Why?

If you were bored out of your skull, did you do anything to correct it? Did you ask for new or additional responsibilities, training, or even a transfer?

Did others know my attitude?

When you were bored, mad, upset, or lost your interest, did you keep your feelings close to the vest or did you broadcast them to anyone with ears? Just remember the cliché "attitudes are like colds, anyone can catch them." You can be branded "poison" if you aren't careful.

Did I follow through? Could people count on me?

Being an idea person is not enough. Did you see projects and promises through to the end, or did you leave things hanging in midstream? Once your word becomes meaningless and people stop relying on you, you're sunk.

Did I understand and meet expectations?

Did you know how you were being judged and what tasks and intangibles were expected of you?

Did I respect my peers and management? If not, was it visible?

You may think that your boss is a clown, and she may well be, but showing open disdain for your boss, management, or coworkers can help speed your progress out the door.

Could I have worked harder?

Everyone has moments when they slack off or give less than 100 percent. Work, like life, has an ebb and flow, periods that are fast, then slow ones. But when it counted, did you give it your all?

Could I have worked smarter?

Working hard is only part of success. Plenty of hard-working people have failed before. Did you work intelligently and make smart choices? Did you think about all of the consequences of your actions and use all of the tools and resources available to you?

Did I "mail it in" or go through the motions? If so, when did it start?

Toward the end of any bad job, or relationship, you start to go through the motions. Did you just show up and make it through the day to collect a check? If so, what triggered this attitude for you? What would have changed your outlook?

Did I procrastinate?

Everyone waits to the last minute occasionally, but was it a habit for you? Did it prevent you from meeting deadlines? Did it affect the quality of your work or cause you to lose credibility? Did your procrastination prevent others from doing their jobs effectively or cause them to look bad?

Did I trust the wrong people?

Did you place trust in someone and get burned? It happens to everyone at some point. Did you share information with the wrong person, who leaked it or used it against you, or did you count on someone who didn't keep his or her word?

Did I champion, support, or introduce a bad idea, program, or person?

Sometimes picking the wrong horse can weigh you down like a boulder around your neck. If the person, program, or idea you supported is out of favor, sometimes so are you. Were your allegiances placed correctly?

Did I produce quality work?

Were you good at what you did, or were you sloppy? Was your work consistently returned to you to do over or correct? Did you frequently have mistakes in your work?

Did I go beyond expectations?

Did you do only what was asked of you, or did you try to anticipate other people's needs, do more than what was asked, or go the extra mile to get the job done properly?

Was I a self-starter, or did I wait for someone to give me directions or tell me what to do?

Did you wait for someone to tell you what to do or give you a project, or did you look for something to do and for ways to contribute and to improve your performance? If this applies to you, you should check out a great book by Bob Nelson, *Don't Just Do What I Tell You . . . Do What Needs to Be Done*. We should all take that to heart.

Did I show initiative and come up with new ideas, or was I waiting to follow the lead of others?

Did you ever come up with a new idea, start a project on your own, or suggest a different or better way to do things? Or did you let others stick their necks out and then ride their coattails?

Did I spend too much time socializing?

We spend over half of our waking day at work. Sometimes we spend more time with our coworkers than with our families, so it is natural that work would become a social outlet. But did you spend a disproportionate amount of time wandering the office from cube to cube, in the break room, smoking in front of the building, or on the phone with your friends? It may have never affected your productivity, but management can take a mental snapshot as they walk around. They may not see the whole picture, but perception is reality. If you are socializing every time they see you, suddenly you are branded the social butterfly.

Did I spend time with people or with a particular group that had a bad reputation with management? Could I have been branded "one of them"?

Your mom was right: "You are known by the company you keep." Did you hang around a person or group of people who had a poor reputation?

Did I allow my personal life to interfere with or affect my work?

Life today can be so hectic, as you try to juggle work, family, friends, and health concerns, that the lines can become blurred over time. Sometimes you simply have to take care of personal items at work. Did you let your personal or home life take over your work life? Did you not distinguish between the two? Did you frequently use employer time to take care of personal issues? It happens. But did you take it to extremes? Did a personal crisis take away from your concentration or your ability to do your best?

Was I seen as a team player or a selfish person?

How did people view you? Were you seen as someone who worked well with others, was selfless and gave of yourself, or were you perceived as a selfish loner who was in it "for me"?

Did I fail to understand or work the system?

Did you understand how things really were accomplished in your organization?

Did I understand and fit in with the culture?

Organizations, departments, or teams are like families in the sense that each has a different personality, style, and way of doing things. Did your personality mesh with the organization's culture? Did you fit in? Was the company unstructured, loose, and casual, but you require structure and hierarchy? Was it a slow-moving traditional bureaucracy where you felt stifled because you need a faster-paced environment? Did you try to adapt to the culture once you discovered it, or was it just never "you"?

Was I in denial about how I was perceived and about my opportunities?

Were there real opportunities for you there? Was your boss or manager being completely truthful about what your future held or what opportunities existed? Loyalty is an admirable trait . . . but so is pragmatism.

Was I in denial about the company's stability?

Did you keep up with the analyst reports, the news reports about your company's health? Were you aware of the trends or events at your company that indicated something was going on, beyond simple belt-tightening?

Did I let people know what I wanted to do and accomplish?
No one will toot your horn for you. Did you tell people
where you wanted to go and what you wanted to do? Or did
you wait to be "discovered"?

Was I a C Teamer?

*Average means that you are as close to the bottom as you are
to the top.* —*Anonymous*

What is a "C Teamer"? In sports these are your third-string
players. They are good enough to make the team, but not
good enough to start. In the working world C Teamers aren't
incompetent or at the bottom of the barrel, but they certainly
aren't setting any world records or climbing the corporate
ladder either.

C Teamers get mediocre results and are not thought of as
leaders or people who inspire others. In the best of times, they
are thought of as the good soldiers, the grunts. In bad times,
they are deadwood, easy pickings for the corporate ax. The
benchwarmers, slugs, and slackers are easy to pick out anytime, but the C Teamers operate under the radar until a poor
corporate performance, a lagging economy, or simply a new
management team turns the light on, exposing everyone's
faults. Where did you fall?

Did I enjoy this job?
Did you like getting up every day? Did you enjoy getting to
work and seeing the people you worked with? Were you challenged, or at least content? Did you like the prestige associated
with what you did? If not, what did you not like about it? Why
did you stay?

Was I satisfied with the amount of money I made?

Everyone wants to make more money . . . but were you always short or stretched? Were you always griping about how your company never paid much compared to others in your field? Did you ask how you could increase your income? What did you do to make more? Was the potential to earn more available to you, but you just didn't or couldn't take advantage of it?

Did I have the resources or training I needed?

If not, did you ask your employer for them, or attempt to get them on your own?

Did I hold a grudge against or resent the organization or my manager?

Did your attitude poison your work? If so, what could you absolutely not forgive or overlook? Why?

Did I pay attention to what was going on around me?

Did you keep your head buried in the sand like an ostrich, or were you aware of shifts, developments, and advancements that could have affected you? Sometimes, when you keep your nose to the grindstone, it pays to look up every once in a while.

Did I meet my targets, or did I consistently fall short?

When you hit your numbers, was it a rarity or was it routine?

Was I as visible as I needed to be, or did I hide behind my work?

You don't need to be a political creature, but did you go out of your way to at least talk with management or other employees?

Was I visible for the wrong reasons?

When people heard your name, what were they most likely to think of: hard worker, good person, nice, friendly, funny, family oriented, smart, or team player? Or were their first thoughts likely to be one of these: has a temper, selfish, complainer, womanizer, drank too much at the holiday party, comes in late? What do you believe you were known for?

QUESTIONS FOR ENTREPRENEURS

Don't think that this exercise applies only if you worked for someone else. If you were self-employed and are now staring at the carcass of what was your company, ask yourself the following:

- ◇ Did I wait too long before pulling the plug or closing the doors?
- ◇ Did I manage people well?
- ◇ Did I manage money well?
- ◇ Did I partner with the right people and organizations?
- ◇ Did I move too fast or too slow?
- ◇ Did I hire well?
- ◇ Did I conduct enough research?
- ◇ Was I aggressive enough/conservative enough?
- ◇ Did I focus hard enough on the right things?
- ◇ Was I open-minded or single-minded? Did I listen to other people, or did I have to be right?

Experience is the hardest kind of teacher. It gives you the test first and the lesson afterward. —*Anonymous*

"I Want a Do Over"

If you ever played schoolyard football, street hockey, or kick-ball on the playground as a kid, you are familiar with the concept of the "do over." Usually when you screw up, make an error, or blow a play you scream, "Do over!" and it is like a free time-out that stops the play and gives you a chance to correct yourself. I only wish that as an adult, there were "do overs." Wouldn't it be great to have a second chance to get it right?

Unfortunately, you don't get such "do overs" or "mulligans" in your career. But you do have a chance to learn from mistakes and make corrections for the future.

Now that you have had a chance to evaluate which circumstances and actions were in and out of your control, what have you learned? Does this evaluation change your perspective or answer questions as to perhaps why you are in your current situation? Could you have handled any of these things differently? Would it have made a difference?

I know that the lists of questions in the Comeback Exercises are quite lengthy. And while some of these things may not directly apply to you or your job, these are many of the factors that ultimately determine whether you are effective, successful, and desirable to an employer. They represent the difference between those people employers fight to keep and those who are allowed to leave, shown the door, or given a pink slip.

What Have I Learned from This?

This taught me a lesson, but I'm not sure what it is.
—*John McEnroe after a loss*

As you asked yourself these questions, did you start to notice recurring patterns or trends in your career and work life? Had any of this happened before? Were you able to identify any weaknesses or circumstances that you suspect have derailed you in the past? Are you repeatedly making poor choices? Perhaps the same destructive actions are preventing you from moving ahead, again and again. The problem may not be the organization or your job, but the fact that you keep taking the same baggage from one organization to another.

> **Experience is not what happens to you. It's what you do with what happens to you.** —*Aldous Huxley*

COMEBACK EXERCISE
What I Learned from This

So how do you leave that baggage behind and correct a possibly damaging trend? For this exercise you will need some paper and thirty minutes of uninterrupted time. Start by briefly reviewing the two lists of questions you just answered, about circumstances beyond your control and circumstances under your control or influence.

Next, take a page and describe in detail what you have learned from this experience and what you would do differently in the future. Even if you were a victim of a layoff and you had absolutely no control over it, this review has surely opened your eyes to ways of improving your career and making yourself bulletproof for next time. Write down your mistakes, what happened, what you failed to see or do, what you could improve upon, and what you would look out for next time. But most important, write down how you would correct your mistakes or avoid them in the future.

Just write. Don't overanalyze. Don't overthink. And don't filter your thoughts. Write what your gut feelings are. Just write as much as possible. Spend exactly thirty minutes doing this. At the end of thirty minutes, stop. Walk away.

Wait until the next day and read it again. Only this time you can really think about it. Your next step is to identify several key lessons or themes from what you have written. These are the core lessons that you will take from this setback experience as you move on to your comeback. The number of lessons will be different for everyone. It can be as few as three to as many as ten. (Beyond ten it gets unwieldy.) In developing your key lessons or themes, you should take each lesson and boil it down to one positive action-oriented phrase. For example:

◇ Be first.
◇ Be fast.
◇ Be loud.
◇ Ask for what I want.
◇ Don't think business will come to me, go get it.
◇ I can't do it alone.
◇ Follow through.
◇ Don't be enamored of others or myself.
◇ Be organized and keep immaculate records.

By the way, how did I come up with these particular life lessons? Easy . . . this is my list of "What I learned" during my career comeback. It is a list I have taped on my desk as a reminder of hard-fought lessons, and to ensure that I don't make the same mistakes twice.

Life is a succession of lessons which must be lived to be understood.
—*Helen Keller*

Now that you have reviewed events leading up to this point, hopefully you have learned something about yourself, maybe something you didn't want to know. This exercise may have opened up some very tender wounds and stirred up some extremely strong feelings and emotions.

You might be mad, sad, disappointed, or frustrated. These feelings may be directed at your former employer, your boss or manager, your partner, coworkers, or even yourself. You need to remember that the key thing in looking back is to learn from your past, correct it, and move forward. A problem occurs when you replay the mistakes in your mind, mentally, playing tapes that scream, "I could have," "I should have," "If I'd only . . ." These tapes that you rewind and replay in your head are what keep you from learning, regaining your confidence, and moving forward.

When you catch yourself having a mental conversation like this . . . stop. I mean literally stop right then and there. Stop what you are doing, stand up, sit down, leave the room, change what you are doing, change your scenery—anything to shake your mind off these destructive thoughts and words. These tapes will keep you from moving forward.

So, now that we have stirred up the hornet's nest of emotion and self-destruction, how can we "erase the tape"?

Learn It . . . Then Burn It

Legend has it that in the 1500s, the Spanish explorer Cortés, upon reaching Mexico's eastern shore, ordered his men to burn all of his expedition's ships. All but one. That ship was to return to Spain to report that they had landed and that Cortés had no plan to do anything but succeed.

By burning the ships Cortés was committing himself and his

men to the mission. Turning back would not be an option. The only choice facing Cortés and his men was to move ahead. By burning the ships he eliminated any excuse for wimping out.

These tapes and excuses that you cling to are your ship, your way to retreat and go back to a safe place that you know, rather than move forward. People are funny. We tend to do what is comfortable and easy if it is available to us. Give most people an excuse, an out, a crutch, or someone to blame, and they will use it.

It is only when we refuse to turn back, or have no other option but to move forward, that we begin to see progress. So, how can you push forward before you are left without an option? How can you destroy your tapes and with them the blame, anger, self-pity, and other negative feelings that this setback has caused? I suggest that you take the poison tapes and thoughts that are holding you back and burn them, as Cortés burned his ships. Here is how.

COMEBACK EXERCISE
Burn the Ships

Do one final piece of writing. (Don't worry, it is the last one and I think you will like the outcome of this.) This letter can be to whomever you wish. It may be to your CEO, your boss, or even yourself. For this you need twenty minutes of completely uninterrupted time. That means no kids, no phone, no e-mail, just twenty minutes of time for you. Spend no more than twenty minutes on this. That's it. Use your watch or your oven timer.

When the clock starts ticking you are to start writing everything you have wanted to say to anyone (including yourself) about your setback. You can spew venom as you wish. Yep, you can direct all of your anger, bitterness, disappointment, and fury in one letter.

As before, it is critical that you don't overthink it. Don't analyze it. Just write freely and from your heart. Don't worry if thoughts are unconnected or don't make sense. Don't even worry about spelling or grammar. Your goal is to get as much out of your system and on to the piece of paper in as short an amount of time as possible. You don't want anything remaining inside your head. This exercise is based on the concept of completely unfiltered writing, sometimes referred to as "ideaphoria," only this time you have a topic suggested to you.

Get it all out on the paper. All of the things you would like to say to your manager, boss, coworkers, or even yourself, if that is who you are blaming. Get it onto the paper and out of your system. This is a purging or cleansing that needs to happen. Otherwise you will sabotage your progress because you are hung up on self-pity, revenge, disappointment, or blame. After twenty minutes, drop the pen or walk away from the keyboard. Get outside. Leave the house or apartment. Take a walk. Just be by yourself for a little bit. Go for a run. Calm down. This can be an intense experience, so you don't want to go immediately from this to dinner with your family or to picking up the kids.

Learn to let go. That is the key to happiness.

—*The Buddha*

Later the same day, after you have cooled down, go someplace where you can be alone and read what you have written. Read it once, straight through. Don't edit. Don't make corrections. Read it once and think about it. It is rational? Highly unlikely. Will these thoughts help you to find your stride, get your next job, provide for your family, and/or improve your life? Probably not.

Read the letter again. This will be the last time that you focus on this destructive energy. Once you have read the letter twice and reflected on how these thoughts can do nothing to help you, get back on your feet, take the letter outside, and burn it. Literally. Set it ablaze. Put a match to it. Torch it. Fire it up like a Viking funeral. (Safely, of course. Have some water nearby, just in case.)

As that letter burns, so do your mental tapes, your negative, vengeful, self-pitying, or self-loathing thoughts. No more will you think about those people who "screwed" you or didn't appreciate you or "did this to you." No more will you wish their demise or consider how you will "show them," "face them," or "embarrass them" when you get your life back on track. No more will you beat yourself up for what you did or didn't do. No more will you consider yourself a loser or a failure.

You won't revisit these thoughts or places again. You no longer have any mental crutches to lean on, and nothing to divert your energy. That's important because you will need all of your mental faculties, confidence, and focus as you take the next steps on your comeback. Like Cortés setting his ships ablaze, with this symbolic burning you now have no choice but to move on. There is no looking back. The only course is to forge ahead.

You'll never plow a field turning it over in your mind.

—*Irish proverb*

Will you make mistakes again? Certainly. Will you revert back to your old ways from time to time? Absolutely. Will you backslide or start to play a conversation in your head when things look bleak? Most of us do. The difference is that now that you can identify and recognize the signs, you can stop and correct them. When you catch yourself thinking these thoughts or falling into a destructive conversation or pity party, stop yourself and remember your little bonfire. Refuse to give those thoughts credibility by allowing them to remain in your head for one second longer.

As you complete this step, you have taken a powerful stride forward in your career comeback. Some people never get beyond this point and let the past poison their thoughts and force them into repeating the same mistakes. But you have identified the causes of your setback and identified areas that you can improve upon in the future. This will boost your confidence and help you to be comfortable in communicating and spinning your story in the future.

Now, take a deep breath. You have taken a huge stride and are starting to pick up steam. You have found solid ground and taken care of the immediate emergencies. You have found out what happened and started to take care of yourself. Now let's find out what others need so you can start to take care of the people close to you.

CAREER COMEBACK FUNDAMENTALS
Finding Out What Happened

◇ Look to your immediate past and identify what went wrong before you move forward. Otherwise you will repeat the same mistakes or find yourself in the same type of organization or situation.

◇ Ask yourself if your setback was for reasons beyond your control (layoff or business closure) or whether you could have influenced the decision.

◇ Identify behaviors you can change that might have played a part in your departure.

◇ Write a letter that vents all of your feelings about the situation—all your venom and emotional baggage—and then burn it.

Find Out What Others Need from You

Help me help you.

—From the movie *Jerry Maguire*

D o you know anyone who has been through a major breakup or divorce? Maybe you have gone through one yourself. If so, you know that it can be a nightmare for the people whose relationship is ending. But it is not just the couple who is affected. The decision may be made by the couple, but the "collateral damage" is staggering and far-reaching. There may be children, in-laws, parents, siblings, nieces, and nephews whose lives are dramatically changed. Mutual friends and acquaintances are eventually forced to choose sides. My point is simply that a breakup does not just impact the two people in the relationship. Others are affected and must adjust accordingly.

What does this have to do with your career setback? Everything. While you may have been the one this has happened to, the people around you are directly and indirectly affected almost as much as you are.

Yeah, I know . . . shouldn't we be paying attention to *your* needs? We will. But unless you are a hermit (who only has a volleyball named Wilson to talk to) or just a purely selfish S.O.B., you know that the earth doesn't revolve around you. Although it certainly feels like it, you are not alone in your comeback. You are taking others along for the ride whether they want to come or not. Your situation doesn't just affect you; it touches the lives of everyone around you, and they are dealing with feelings, concerns, fears, and anxieties of their own. Yes, you are in pain. Yes, you have experienced a loss. But there are other people with whom you share your life and whom your actions directly influence. To make a successful comeback you will need their love and support. But it is a two-way street. You have to give in order to get. You can't control how others treat you, so instead of worrying about what others can do for you, let's look at something you actually can control—how you deal with other people by giving them what they need.

What Your Family Needs

Don't Be Afraid to Talk About It: Silence Doesn't Mean It Didn't Happen

"If a tree falls in the forest and no one hears it, does it still make a noise?" While that has long been one of the great existential debates, when it comes to a career setback, there is no debate at all. If you don't talk about your situation, and pretend that life is going on as normal, if you ignore the fact that you're hurt or angry, does that mean that everything is okay? In short, no.

Each of us wants to appear strong for our family and loved ones. It doesn't matter if you are a man or a woman, you want to be the rock, the steady unflappable force that everyone else

Only about eighteen months after earning his MBA, Aaron was part of a major reorganization and lost his job. He and his wife, who were newlyweds, agreed not to let their parents know what had happened. "I didn't want them worrying about us or thinking that we couldn't take care of ourselves." Aaron managed to avoid telling his parents for weeks, until his brother, whom he had confided in, let the secret slip. "My mom was upset that I would keep something from her, and my dad was disappointed because he could have helped us along rather than letting us struggle for the past few months."

can depend on and look to for support. But when there is a crisis, clamming up and becoming silent is not a sign of strength.

You don't spare your family any pain by keeping things bottled up inside, changing the subject, or refusing to discuss the realities of the situation. In fact, it takes strength to let other people share your pain and help you through it. Events like this have the ability to either bring you together or tear you apart. If you establish open communication in the beginning, the little things don't become big things. Remember, bad news is not like wine, it doesn't get better with age.

I fell victim to the "strong and silent" myth during my comeback. Using some backward machismo logic, I was under the impression that I was helping my family by remaining a quiet pillar of strength and projecting an image that said, "Everything will be all right. I'm in control."

Inside I was a train wreck as I wrestled with saving my company versus getting a job. But at home and with the people close to me, I felt it was my obligation, my duty, and my cross to bear to remain silent and thus shield them from anything bad that could happen.

Fortunately I'm lucky enough to have a wife who is smart enough and strong enough for both of us when we need it. It was she who spoke first and helped to clear the air and open communication. She was the one to let me know that I didn't have to be quiet to be strong. Our open communication got things moving forward in the right direction and eliminated a great deal of pressure and guesswork. Our marriage is a partnership, and as we go on life's quest together, this just happened to be another part of it that we would get through . . . together.

"Enough About You, What Does It Mean to Me?"

Everyone views the world through his or her own eyes. It's not selfish; it is just human nature. Even though the career setback has happened to *you*, the people close to you will instinctively think, "How will this affect me?"

Everyone views it differently. Your spouse or partner may wonder what this means to your finances and your dreams of retirement or remodeling the house, or wonder if he or she will have to go back to work or if you will lose the house. Your kids will wonder if they will have to change schools, move, or leave their friends. If your kids are older they might be concerned about college or how it will impact their social status. Your parents might be thinking about what your setback will mean to their own retirement if they have to help you out financially or if you have to move in with them. They may be concerned that they will have to delay or alter their retirement plans.

Remember that you aren't the only one who may be concerned or scared. Ask your partner what his or her greatest con-

Dottie, a sixtysomething working widow, was beside herself when not one but both of her adult children were laid off. "Obviously I was worried for my kids. I wondered how long it would take them to find something else. I worried what they would do and if they would be able to bounce back from this. But I can't say that I wasn't concerned about my well-being. As a widow approaching retirement age, I was scared that my kids would have to move back in with me. I would give them my last dime if they needed it, but what would a lengthy job search do to my finances? I was planning to retire next year and suddenly I was faced with putting that on hold to help them."

cerns or fears are about the current situation. When they answer, don't immediately respond. Allow them to list all of their concerns and explain or elaborate if they wish. Each person's thoughts are valid, even if you feel they are trivial, so don't dismiss them. This will help you to know the triggers that can upset your partner, so you can address them. When possible, answer and address each fear or concern as directly and honestly as possible. Let the other person know how you plan to address each concern. If you don't know or have no answer, say so.

Agree on a Course of Action

Just as these events force you to evaluate your career (as we did in Step 2), you are also forced to take stock of your family's needs, goals, and expectations. After the initial shock has worn off, one of the first things that you should do is sit down with your partner or spouse or your entire family and agree on a course of action.

This is a conversation that you should plan for and schedule. This is not something that you spring on anyone or start at an inopportune time, such as when you are getting ready in the morning, going out on Saturday night, or just before going to bed when you are tired.

Here are a few areas that you should discuss and come to an agreement on:

◇ What does this mean to your family? Is this the answer to a prayer? Is it an opportunity to change direction or make a change for yourself or your family that you have been putting off?

◇ Are you willing to relocate if necessary?

◇ Is your spouse willing to go back to work if it comes to that?

◇ Where do you need to cut expenses or change your lifestyle?

◇ How will things change around the house?

◇ Are you going to pursue a similar job? Do you need to take something in the interim to make ends meet? How long will you try to get "the right job" before you compromise and accept other work?

Your decisions aren't set in stone. Your course of action should remain fluid as events and circumstances change. The point is to have you and your family on the same page as you progress. It is far better to come up with a plan at the beginning (and not have to use it) rather than try to wing it as you go.

Once you have come to some sort of conclusion or decision, it might be a good idea to gather everyone in the family who might be affected, including children. This way you can

Julie was devastated when she lost her lucrative sales job. But when she and her husband took stock of their family situation after the layoff, they determined that this layoff might just be a blessing in disguise. While Julie's income was attractive, the travel and stress were taking a toll on the family, including her two small kids. Together Julie and her family decided that it would be best for her to find a part-time job that did not require travel so she could focus her energies on being a stay-at-home mom. "I can go back when the kids are older and the economy turns around, but right now we can afford it if I cut back, and I want to be there while my kids are this age. I wouldn't have even considered it unless this happened."

Alan had already put one daughter through college at a prestigious and expensive liberal arts college and was preparing to send his youngest daughter to school after she graduated high school in the spring. But shortly after losing his position as a corporate vice president, Alan faced the prospect of telling his youngest daughter that her college plans might have to be altered or even postponed. "My daughter is a good kid, but she was crushed and felt that it was incredibly unfair that her sister was able to go to a top school, and she's being forced to go to a local school or wait a year. She thinks this is happening to her. I didn't expect her to understand."

Sharon, 44, whose husband has been unemployed for over seven months, says, "It is difficult watching my husband go through this. Society seems to put more pressure on men. I just try to keep him motivated by helping him keep things in perspective."

clear the air, learn what their thoughts and concerns are, and communicate your plan. Communication is key to preventing problems at home.

Be Optimistic . . . but Realistic

There are a couple of universal truths. The first is that everyone thinks they have a sense of humor. The second is that everyone thinks it won't take them long to find another job. No one, not even the great and powerful job search experts and prognosticators, can predict how long it will actually take you to land a job or what you will encounter along the way. (My career comeback took four months . . . and I know what I'm doing.)

Optimism is important, but so is pragmatism. You don't want to be the prophet of doom but you want to give a positive yet realistic assessment of your progress, your prospects, and where you stand financially and emotionally. The people close to you are as emotionally involved in your job search as you are. They rise with the highs and sink with the lows. They get as excited as you do when you have an interview or get a promising lead, and are equally crushed and disappointed when it doesn't work out or you receive a rejection letter.

It is crucial for you to temper everyone's expectations, as well as your own. Be positive, enthusiastic, and hopeful, but don't give anyone false hope or inflate how something appears because you don't want anyone else to worry. Be realistic. If an interview went really well and looks promising, say so. If you truly feel that it was a bust, or if a lead or contact wasn't as helpful as you had expected, that is all right too.

Show That You Care and Are Doing Something to Correct the Situation

One career expert advises you to tell your family that your "periods of inactivity" are actually reflection, and that you should ask them not to be harsh with you as you regroup. I don't know about you, but I don't think my wife would have taken it too well if during my comeback, she had walked in to find me on the couch, with the Cheetos and the remote control . . . "reflecting." Second only to actually finding a job, your family wants you to be actively looking for a job.

What drives friends and family crazy is when it appears that you have given up, thrown in the towel, or, worse, are waiting

> April's husband had recently been laid off, but had worked hard at his job search for the past month and managed to generate some income through a couple of contract jobs. One sunny day, he called April at work and sheepishly asked, "Would you be upset if I went to the pool this afternoon?" April said, "Of course not, you have been working harder on this search than you did when you were working full-time." It was because her husband had exhibited drive and action that April had no problem with him taking a day off, which we all need from time to time.

Jessica was worried about her husband, Larry, after he was laid off from his job as a network engineer. After three months of actively looking for another position with no results, Larry became withdrawn and began staying around the house all of the time and putting all of his effort into the yard and the house. According to Jessica, "I don't want to be a nag or pick on him, but all he does is work on the yard. I'm glad that he is working on the house . . . but he needs to be working on getting a job."

for the stars and moon to align themselves so the "right" opportunity can jump up and bite you on your rear end. Too many job seekers overthink the situation, overprepare, or simply look for every excuse for why now is not a good time to do anything. This includes sitting on your butt as you wait for the recruiter to call, for the holidays to be over, for your contact to get back from vacation, for the economy to change, for budgets to be approved, for you to get an introduction, or for monkeys to fly. In lieu of your getting an offer, they want to see some action. This doesn't mean that you can't take a break, though.

"Why Aren't You More Upset?"

How do you feel when someone says something rude to your spouse or picks on your child? What do you want to do when someone says something bad about your parents or a sibling? If you're like most people, you want to step in there and protect your loved one. You want to take up for them and fight for them. You want to right a wrong. Maybe give them a piece of your mind . . . or better yet, a fat lip. "No one treats my family that way." In Texas we call these "fighting words."

Now think of this fact and put yourself in the position of your spouse, partner, parent, or other family member or close friend. They are downright mad as hell that you were treated so poorly and have been let go. They are furious that after making sacrifices for the company, this is how you have been treated. They are mad because they know how talented you are and how hard you work and they can't believe that a company or manager could be so blind and stupid. They are angry that they too have had to sacrifice family time, weekends, and late nights and put up with missed events, relocations, and broken promises only to be paid back like this. Like you, they feel betrayed, cheated, and disappointed.

Stoicism and calm are not what they need or want from you. As strange as it sounds, they want to see that you are upset enough that you will do something about it. I'm not talking about grinding your teeth, breaking furniture, or raging in anger, but they want to know that you are not taking it lying down.

They Deserve to Be Angry Too

The people close to you know that you certainly don't want to be in this situation, and that it may not be your fault. But that doesn't change the fact that they are upset. They might be furious but choose to keep it inside or hidden from you. It might take them a while to say anything, but when they do don't be surprised if they blow like Mount Vesuvius.

Let them vent, yell, scream, cry, whatever makes them feel better. Don't interrupt them, make excuses, apologize, or rationalize with them. Let the other person get things off of his or her chest. You can avoid major flare-ups if you communicate frequently and know what each other's expectations, fears, and feelings are.

You Don't Have a Monopoly on Stress

We all can be selfish, self-centered, and even self-pitying, but during a crisis these qualities can be magnified. While your life may seem to have temporarily stopped, it continues for everyone else around you.

The people close to you are usually tuned in to your situation and pretty sensitive about dumping on you. But they too have their share of disappointments that go with everyday life. Some may seem trivial compared to yours, but it is important that you give them the freedom to share these things with you. They might be reluctant to share disappointments with you unless you give them the green light to do so.

Take the focus off yourself. Your situation shouldn't prevent you from being there emotionally for your spouse, or from serving as an outlet for them to share their everyday challenges. Ask how their day was. Listen attentively. Let them know that they can talk to you. And when someone does tell you about a problem or complaint, don't turn it around and talk about yourself. Be there for them, and they will be there in return when you need it.

Fight Fair—Attack the Situation or Event, Not the Other Person

You both are likely mad at the situation rather than each other, so try to keep things in perspective and not turn your anger into a personal assault. If there is a blowup or argument, make sure to fight fair. This means sticking to the facts and to what your own feelings are. Don't blame or use accusatory language or phrases like "You did this," "You make me feel . . . " or "If you would only." I'd say that it would be a safe bet to stay away from the word "you" in general. Self-esteem is likely to be running low and tensions high, so having a knock-down, drag-out fight can result in nothing positive.

Your Partner Defends You More Than You Will Ever Realize

Does it bug you when people are constantly asking, "Have you found anything yet?" "How is the search going?" It can get old after a point, especially if it is taking a while or there is no progress to report. However, the number of people who actually say something to you pales in comparison to the number of people who ask your spouse, family, or loved one these questions.

The fact is that you will never know exactly how many people ask and inquire because your spouse or partner acts as a bodyguard, fielding questions from people who care about you or are simply inquisitive but don't want to bother you. Instead of bombarding you with a barrage of questions, your spouse shields and defends you by answering, "No, not yet." "He has a few leads." "He has an interview lined up." He or she is confronted with your job loss every time someone asks about you.

But it is not just questions that your spouse or partner shields you from. Your spouse takes the brunt of comments from every armchair career guru, nosy neighbor, or pushy mother-in-law with an opinion on why you aren't gainfully employed yet. Most job seekers who are in a relationship never know how much pressure their partner endures, because the partner won't speak up, and they shouldn't. They take a bullet

> Felicity, 32, says, "I adore my husband and completely support him. I know how talented he is and see how hard he is working, but I worry that others don't always see that. When my family asks how the search is going, I find myself being overly optimistic or even lying about the way things are. I just don't want them to judge him unfairly."

for you every time someone asks about you, and you've never known . . . until now.

Now that you know this, you can start to understand that the situation is hard on partners and spouses in ways that you never see or think about. What can you do about it? Not much. You can't change it. We will always defend the ones we love. But every once in a while, a simple "thank you for supporting me and believing in me" can be the best reward for a spouse . . . outside of your getting a job, of course.

Make a Contribution

While you might not be able to contribute financially, you can contribute in other ways that can go a long way toward relieving any pressure around the house. You might take over the family shopping, run the car pool, cook a meal, help your kids with homework, contribute an extra session of watching the kids, or get around to those home repairs that you have been putting off. You might even save money by getting rid of the yard guy and mowing your own lawn. These are extremely simple things that you have control over and that demonstrate that you are making an effort to fulfill your role as a family member or partner . . . no paycheck required.

I've spoken with a lot of job seekers (and their agitated families) who choose to play the victim or feel that their trauma has earned them an extended vacation or free pass from family duties.

Don't think, "I can't be bothered, I need all of my time to work on my job search." Sure, you need to focus your time and energy on your search, but let's be realistic. If you spend every waking moment on your job search, and you haven't found something yet, then you aren't being very effective. You can spare an hour or two to help out and make things easier on everyone.

Most people fight and argue about the little things around the house that bug them: the trash, the clothes, the dishes, and the way you roll your socks. When there is stress from a real and significant event like a job loss, then the insignificant things can quickly become a lighting rod. Everyone surrounding you is making adjustments or sacrifices during this period. There are bound to be some tasks that you are called on to perform that don't usually fall in your area of responsibility or expertise. If so, "suck it up." Do whatever it takes to make things work. You will be stunned at how those little things relieve the pressure.

On the other hand, the fact that you are spending more time at home and helping out more than usual is not a license to make you an indentured servant. In fact, you may resent being forced into this new role, especially if others are taking the fact that you are at home for granted. If you have ever worked from home, you know what I'm talking about. Your spouse comes home at the end of the day, looks at the messy house, and says, "What is up with the mess? You were here all day, why didn't you do anything?"

The best way to avoid any conflict is for you to contribute, but to establish boundaries and expectations. If it gets out of hand, then you will simply have to leave the house or tell others that you are "off limits" during working hours. Tell them that they should think of you as a normal working person and that you can't be disturbed unless it is an emergency. It is not a pretty conversation, but it's one that will help everyone in the long run.

Respect Your Family's Routine and Space

It has been said that "Good fences make good neighbors." What does that have to do with you? Simply put, your family has a routine and *you* are the one disrupting it.

Let me explain. While you were working you might have thought how wonderful it would be to take time off and spend more time with the family. Well, now that you have inadvertently gotten your wish and are at home "all of the time, day after day," the truth is . . . you are starting to get on everyone's nerves.

Your spouse and kids have a routine. They have boundaries and a system that existed long before you started spending more time at home. Now that you are around, you have disrupted it.

Change is inevitable, but realize that you are throwing a wrench in the works. Don't take it badly or let your feelings get hurt. I'm sure that they love you and would rather have you there than at the office or on a plane . . . at least for now. But they simply aren't used to having you around.

This is not to say that you should let the kids run wild and scream while you are trying to make calls, or let them monopolize the Web connection searching NickJr.com when you should be sending e-mail or searching job boards, but you should respect their boundaries and routines.

After Peter, a fiftysomething corporate vice president, was laid off, he thought that he would use this opportunity to spend more time with his wife. He kept asking her to meet him for lunch, but she always seemed to be running errands or had plans with her friends. One day Peter finally asked her why she wouldn't make time to have lunch with him, and she said, "Honey, I married you for richer, for poorer, for sickness and for health . . . but not for lunch. You're getting in the way of my routine."

Claiming the kitchen table as your personal workspace, as if this were the Oklahoma Land Run, can be overwhelming for everyone. Find out what everyone's routine is and what their needs are. You should discuss what you need as well.

If you don't have a home office or spare bedroom, perhaps you can create a specific workspace and designate the area within certain boundaries as a "kid-free" or "quiet" zone where you can be uninterrupted between certain hours. The extra time you now have with your family is nice, but this is not a vacation.

With you at home all of the time now, the novelty can wear off pretty quickly. Your focus has been on the office and work for a long time, and now your attention is on them. It can cause some stress. You may be privy to things that you were never aware of before, now that you have more opportunity to notice things like how your kids dress, what they eat, or how they communicate with each other or with you. Your spouse may have a system or certain rules with the kids. Do not undermine his or her authority or routine.

Don't hover or be a constant nuisance. Give them the space they need, even if it means going to the library or

Starbucks for a while. If you have another location or an office you can go to, possibly through your outplacement firm, you might take advantage of it for everyone's sanity.

But Don't Be a Hermit or Ignore Them Either, and Use Your Time Wisely

Some career gurus suggest that you take advantage of this situation, do the things you've never had time to do before, such as take a class, learn a language, or work on your relationship.

After shutting my company down, I found myself conducting my job search from a home office located upstairs. I had always loved the home office before this, but now it felt like an isolation chamber. Previously I had other people around me and I was able to shout out what I was thinking, share good news, or vent when necessary.

Now I was in my home-based veal-feeding pen, armed with a phone, a computer, and an Internet connection. Whenever I received a positive e-mail or phone call, in my excitement I would bolt downstairs and share my joy with my wife, regardless of what she was doing at that exact moment. I would stand there as eager as a little kid, or a puppy who is about to pee on the rug, completely oblivious to the fact that she was in the middle of reading or watching a show, or in the shower. She would eventually smile and say, "That's great honey," as she shot me a look that said, "Good, now go back upstairs and leave me alone."

Get real. (As if my wife and I sat around drinking flavored cof-
fees at 2:00 P.M. as we worked on our relationship and discussed world events.) Even if you have a great relationship and
a bag full of money to tide you over, this is still a stressful time.
You may have more free time than you had in the past, but you
might not be in a mood or position to enjoy it.

However, if you have been logging more time on airplanes
than at home in the past few years, then this might be a chance
for you to slow down and remember why you are working so
hard. If your finances can stand it, this can serve as a mini-
sabbatical that gives you a chance to reconnect with your family. This is a unique opportunity that you otherwise would
never take, unless you were forced.

As a family, create a list of four or five major things that you
would like to accomplish, see, or do together. These can be
the trips or campouts that you all never have time for. You
might take a set amount of time off together—a month, three
months, whatever you can afford.

This is great if you can afford it, but how many of us have
that luxury? Let's look at a scaled-down economy version. You
might not be able to take a sabbatical for weeks or months at a
time, but just about everyone can afford to take a couple of
hours or a day to devote to someone else.

Create a personal list of things that you want to do during
this period. I suggest that they be small things: "pick up my
child from school two days a week"; "have lunch with my son
once a week"; "eat dinner as a family"; "take my kid to soccer
practice"; "make my girlfriend or boyfriend dinner once a
week." Make it a point to spend a portion of your time with
your child or your family. Use part of your time to take care of
things around the house. Use your time wisely. Once you're
working again, you might even see this time as a missed opportunity—so don't miss out.

What Kids Need

Don't Fool Them

Kids are perceptive. They can sense things and can pick up on stress or changes in the environment. They notice if things are different around the house or if Mommy or Daddy is around much more than before. Some people advocate not telling your kids what is happening. "Why should we worry them?" I totally disagree. I think that you should tell your kids what is going on, but do so in age-appropriate terms. You don't have to go into great detail. They can't differentiate between "lay-off" and "firing." With young kids your explanation can be as simple as "Mommy is going to get a new job."

Ask if they have questions. You will be surprised. My son, who was four at the time, was full of questions like "What happened to your old office?" "Where did it go?" "What happened to the people?" It was important to him, because he had spent time there, played there, and knew the people who worked for me.

Teenagers and adult children can logically understand the business reasons behind what has happened, but besides being concerned for themselves, they are concerned for you. They may have never seen you in this type of situation before, and they hope that you are able to come back. Failing to level with them or trying to shield them can only lead to a breakdown in trust later on.

Kids Need Stability

What kids need more than anything at a time like this is to know that something in their life is stable, and often that stability comes from you or your family. Reassure your kids that your work has changed, but your family has not. You still love them and care for them. You are not going anywhere. If possible, tell your kids together with your spouse. It is important that they see you together and that you appear as a stable, unified force. "We as a family will make it. We will survive." You can reassure them that while some things may change, the family is going to remain together. Let them know how they can help.

Younger Kids Take Things Literally

Young kids have no frame of reference for something like this and don't know what it means. They don't know how serious it is. That is why it is critical that you communicate with your child and control the type of information he or she receives. If they don't receive any information, then they will fill the void with their own thoughts.

One day my six-year-old daughter overheard a conversation in which someone used the phrase "He was fired." She asked me what that meant and without going into great detail, I told her that it meant someone lost his job. She seemed extremely upset by this and asked, "Daddy, does it hurt when they are fired?" It turns out that Samantha thought that when someone is "fired," they are literally set ablaze. She was scared that someone's poor daddy was going to be marched out of the office and set on fire, and she didn't want it to happen to me. Talk about a vivid imagination. The point is that kids take things very literally.

Older Kids Worry About Themselves

Adolescent and teenage kids understand what is going on and know the severity of it, but their concerns are more personal. How will your career setback change their life? They are worried about things like moving, changing schools, leaving their friends, loss of material possessions and social status, or having to delay, alter, or even postpone their college choices.

Grown Kids Worry About You

If your kids are grown, they understand much of what you are going through and may have experienced a setback of their own. Their concerns are more about your well-being and are likely to be much more pragmatic. They may have never seen you dejected and wonder how you will cope. Will you be able to keep a positive outlook? Will you be able to find another position? What will this mean for your retirement? Will they need to help you out financially?

Your Actions Will Teach Your Kids
How to Deal with Adversity

You are setting an important precedent for your kids. While this certainly isn't how you planned to teach your kids a lesson, you have an incredible opportunity to teach them about adversity and comeback. They will watch how you handle this situation. They will see if you are resilient or if you let it defeat you, whether you let the stress overwhelm you and you take it out on those closest to you or if you act with composure and channel your frustration into positive action. They will see if you maintain a positive attitude and fight through problems head-on or if you run from them.

This process can be a learning experience for you and your kids, especially if you have teenage or older kids who may see this as a breakdown in the system of hard work or fairness. Hard work and loyalty are admirable qualities that we try to exhibit and teach to our kids, but when they see your hard work and loyalty rewarded by your losing your job, then why should they work so hard at school or anything else? "Why does it matter? Look what happened to my parents."

You may question the fairness of the system as well, but your challenge is to show your kids that this can't keep you down or prevent you from moving forward. You are teaching them by example. Showing your kids that setbacks and disappointments occur at all points in life and can happen to anyone teaches them a valuable lesson, but more valuable is your ability to teach them that obstacles can be overcome. Lead by example.

> **They may forget what you said, but they will never forget how you made them feel.**
> —*Carl Buehner*

What Friends and Acquaintances Need

Be Cheery . . . but Not Too Cheery

Have you ever known a couple that appeared perfect on the outside, always happy, smiling, and never, ever fighting or arguing? You know, the type of couple that makes everyone jealous because they have this seemingly perfect relationship. Then you get the surprise news that they are getting a divorce. Suddenly all sorts of salacious details come to the surface about

I'M SINGLE, DON'T HAVE KIDS, AND DON'T HAVE FAMILY NEARBY. WHAT DOES THIS MEAN TO ME?"

A lot of people who are single or divorced and who don't have any family nearby view their close friends as family. They might be there for emotional support, to assist with job leads, and to perform many of the same functions a family member would. The main difference is that your friends don't rely on you financially.

Your newly unstable employment situation can put a severe crimp in your social life and spending habits, and this can affect your friendships. Where in the past you and your buddies or group of friends would go out to dinner, plan weekend trips, pay for each other's drinks, plan birthday events, or exchange gifts, you may have to bow out because you are watching your pennies or you simply can't afford it.

It may be embarrassing, but your close friends will (or at least should) understand. The toughest part is stepping up and telling someone that you can't afford to do something. You might consider offering an alternative. If your social life once revolved around going out, get creative and come up with cheaper solutions.

Like family, what your friends need from you is honesty. If you can't do something, say so. A career comeback teaches you a lot about who your friends really are and about their character. You will identify who sticks with you and who leaves when things aren't fun, and you are no longer buying a few rounds on the weekend.

the problems they had and how the "perfect" relationship was a facade. The point is that appearances can be deceiving.

Be honest and authentic with your friends. If you are sincerely up, then be up. Shout it loud, shout it proud, and let others know that you are getting back on track. But a career setback can dampen the most hard-core optimist. Putting on a "happy face" or pretending that everything is "A-OK" if you are crumbling inside doesn't do anyone any good. You owe it to the people around you to give them an accurate gauge of where you are.

Another reason you don't want to give the false impression that you are on top of the world is because it can backfire on you. Your friends will admire an honest assessment of what is happening, how you are doing, and what your prospects are. False bravado is a guaranteed way to make sure that no one will help you. People will begin to think, "Oh, he is doing great, what does he need from me? He has it under control." "Oh, things are great. Really? Well, that's good. I'll stop asking."

Be Present and in the Moment for Them

It is entirely too easy to let something like this consume you to the point where you are oblivious to everything around you. You can become self-absorbed to such a degree that you shut everyone else out. Not only is this destructive and counterproductive for you; it inadvertently hurts those around you as well. While you aren't intentionally isolating yourself, your lack of attention and concentration is pushing people away.

Snap out of it and get out of your own head. Life is going on all around you and you are missing it. Constant worry and anxiety is alienating the people you care for and are working so hard to take care of. Take time to notice the small things, the little

Shortly after I made the decision to close my company, my head was everywhere, except where I was. Part of the time my thoughts were filled with "What could I have done? What should I have done? If I had only . . . " The other half of the time my mind was riddled with questions that weren't getting me closer to my goal, but were digging me deeper into the hole and taking me further from the people who needed me. "What will others think?" "What if I don't find something?" It was a constant barrage of "what ifs" . . . and in the meantime, or in "real time," I had three people who needed me to be present and accounted for both physically and mentally.

I found everything a nuisance or a distraction. I didn't want to play with my kids. I didn't want to go out with friends. Even when I was alone or out with my wife, my head was on the job hunt and the "what ifs." I couldn't think about the upcoming birth of my third child because I was completely self-absorbed and consumed with what would become of me.

Was I effectively seeking employment twenty-four hours a day? Of course not. But I was being a worrying jerk twenty-four hours a day and robbing the people who cared for me and needed me of my time and attention. I was in denial. I was determined to do what was best for them, but what was best for them was for me to calm down and put that same intensity into the job hunt during the day and then leave it alone. Fortunately, the birth of my second son halfway through my comeback made me wake up and realize where I needed to give my attention.

wonders around you that God puts before you every day. Enjoy the things and the people around you right now. I know that you have much on your mind. Serious concerns are weighing you down. I've been there and I know that it is not easy to flip the switch and turn your thoughts to something or someone else at a time like this. But I'm telling you from experience, don't worry constantly about what you don't have or what you need to do, or you will end up missing the joy of what you do have right now.

> **Life is like a coin. You can spend it any way you wish, but you can only spend it once.** —*Miguel de Cervantes*

Ask Others for Their Advice or Opinion

Your spouse or partner and your friends want to be included. This is happening to them as much as it is you, but they are powerless. You are the captain of this ship and they are along for the ride. At least let them help navigate. Ask their opinion. Seek their advice. Use them as a sounding board or as a resource to review your material or help you practice your interviews. Include them as much as they want to be included. They may not take you up on it, but you should offer to include them.

Accuracy Counts, Not Drama

> **Just the facts, Ma'am.** —*Detective Joe Friday*, Dragnet

We are a culture that loves the scoop, the dish, the gossip, or the inside story. We are also a culture that loves to recount all of the drama and blow-by-blow details of seemingly everyday events. Everyone at some point has probably spiced up a story a little bit. A car cuts you off in a parking lot to snag a prime space and you get mad, maybe honk your horn and call the person a jerk—to your steering wheel. But when you tell your friends what happened, the story is dramatized with great detail and your minor honk is translated into a self-righteous display that almost came to blows. Often when people describe their departure from an organization, it can take on the qualities of a fisherman's tale of the one that got away.

Revisionist history, embellishment, and drama can infect the story when you are talking about the events surrounding your departure. Don't let it happen. Stick to the facts, don't embellish, overstate, or dramatize. There are a couple of reasons for this. The first is simply that no one cares as much as you do. They care about you, but they really aren't interested in all of the gory details. Chances are that they don't know the players involved or any of the history or back story. It means more to you than it ever will to them.

The second reason you want to stick to the facts is because every time you retell the extended story, you are reliving it all over again. All of the emotions and feelings that you have suppressed or forgotten rise to the surface and hold you back from moving ahead. Remember when we "burned the ships" in Step 2? This is why. You can't keep reliving the past. It is like someone who has a breakup and is still talking about the other person many months later.

Encourage Others to Share Good News with You

Have you ever had some really good news that you wanted to share with a friend who was going through a rough time, but you didn't out of concern that it would make that person feel bad? You hold off sharing your happiness or good fortune with these people because you think that it might be considered bad timing or poor taste. Or it could be that your friend is a complete buzz kill. We've all known people who love to revel in their own misery so much that they tend to suck the light and joy from anything positive anyone else has to say. As a result, people stop sharing good news with them.

Here is a remarkably simple, age-old exercise that you might try with your partner, family, or friends. It's been said that with our rushed, activity-filled, dual-income society, no one sits down for family dinner anymore. I can attest that with three little ones, we are sometimes lucky to get them fed without it turning into a three-ring circus. But even if you can't do it every day, you might establish one night a week to sit down together and have dinner or make a phone call so that everyone can share two or three good things that happened that week. That goes for you too. Force yourself to find something good.

You can be so focused on the negative or what is not working that you forget happiness and goodness are all around you, you just aren't looking for them. And if you have teenagers or a smart-aleck kid, don't let them take this lightly. Make everyone find something of substance to discuss. This exercise is a reminder that you, your friends, and your clan are not cursed or being followed by a black rain cloud. It lets you and the people you care about know that there are good things happening even during a challenging time.

Just as someone might be apprehensive about telling you bad news or dumping their problems on you because of your situation, they may be just as reluctant to share good news with you. The irony is that right now you need all the good news and positive energy you can get. Make it a point to go out of your way to encourage the people close to you to share their happiness, successes, and good news with you. Celebrate their happiness and triumphs, even the small victories. It creates a positive and supportive environment for everyone around you and takes the focus off your disappointment. At times like this a lot of attention and concern is focused on you. People are being your supporters and cheerleaders. Return the favor and show your appreciation by shining the light on them.

> There are two ways of spreading light: to be the candle or the mirror that reflects it.　　　　　—Edith Wharton

> If you don't like the movie, don't attack the screen, change the reel.　　　　　—Dr. Phil McGraw

Friends Are Patient, but They Aren't Your Personal Dumping Ground

Have you ever had a friend who suffered a breakup and just couldn't seem to let it go? Sure, you were there for them initially, but after weeks they were still weepy and angry and everything reminded them of their ex. They just simply refused to make any effort to get better. After a while you wanted to stop being around them, because they were just bringing everyone around them down, but were unwilling to do anything about the situation. The same thing is true with a career setback. Your friends and the people around you will put up with a lot, but everyone has their limits. Here is a primer on how to keep your feelings in check and not cross the line.

It Is Okay to Feel Pain or Disappointment . . . as Long as You Don't Make It a Habit

You've experienced a loss or disappointment. There is no denying it. And no one says it doesn't hurt. You are completely entitled to express pain as you run the gamut of emotions. It is perfectly normal for you to be upset or sad, to cry, scream, or mope. People who know you and love you expect it and will give you some latitude if you aren't yourself one day. But realize that it gets old after a while, especially if you appear unwilling to do anything to help yourself or to let others help you.

It Is Okay to Be Angry . . . as Long as It Motivates You to Do Something Positive

Just as you might feel pain or disappointment, it is not uncommon to drift in and out of anger. You should be angry. You probably deserve to be angry (just as long as it is not vengeful, crazy, violent, psycho anger).

But again, *do not* make a habit of dwelling on any bitterness or resentment you may harbor. Anger can be an extremely effective motivator when used as a call to action. However, when your anger paralyzes you or causes you to focus on what is going wrong or why something didn't happen, then you have a problem. Use your anger in short bursts, to spur you to action and ignite a drive to move from the place where you are.

I suggest running. Pull a Forrest Gump and run to the point of exhaustion. Go to the gym and lift weights as hard as you can, punch a bag, do push-ups or sit-ups until you can't stand it anymore. Get your frustration out somehow so that you are too physically exhausted to remain angry.

It's Okay to Feel Self-Pity . . . for About an Hour

Like a lot of kids, when I was little and I didn't get my way I would stick out my bottom lip and pout or feel sorry for myself. (My wife says I still do it.) After I would sit there for a while, my mom would always ask if I was having a "pity party."

As an adult, nothing entitles you to a pity party like losing your job or running a business into the ground—but the difference is that Mom is not going to be there to get you out of your self-indulgent, self-pitying funk. Like feeling anger and disappointment, it is perfectly normal for you to feel self-pity, but only for about an hour and only if you can snap out of it and start doing something about it.

Bad things happen to all of us, and even the strongest people have moments when they wonder "Why me?" or "Why does God keep doing this to me?" But the bottom line is that no one likes a whiner. The people around you will give you space to wallow for a short period of time, but then it is time to start sending a different message and take some action. You owe it to yourself and to the people you care about. At least with anger you can be mad enough to change things. With disappointment or pain, the hurt can push you to change things. But you can't change anything by feeling sorry for yourself.

CAREER COMEBACK FUNDAMENTALS
Finding Out What Others Need from You

◇   Don't be afraid to talk about what has happened. Silence doesn't mean that it didn't happen.

◇   Agree on a course of action.

◇   The people close to you need communication, not silence or stoicism.

◇   Those close to you view the setback through their own eyes and wonder what it means to them. It affects them almost as much as it does you.

◇   Even though your routine has been disrupted, respect your family's space and routine.

◇   Be optimistic but realistic when communicating with others.

◇   Accuracy counts, not drama. Stick to the facts when communicating what happened.

◇   Life continues. Encourage others to share good news with you.

Step 4

Find Your Support System

*As iron sharpens iron, so one man sharpens
another.*

—Proverbs 27:17

If you have a wreck or your car breaks down on the side of
the road, you may need a tow truck or someone to drive
you home. You might need a mechanic or body shop to
repair your car. You might need your insurance agent to help
file your claim and pay for any damages. You may need a po-
lice officer to settle a dispute. If you are injured you might
even need a doctor . . . or one of those cheesy attorneys on
late-night television who ask "Have you been injured?" C'mon,
if you are in a wreck, you don't simply pop an aspirin, put the
car in your garage, and try to fix it yourself, do you? You need
people, institutions, and resources to help get you back on the
road.

This is no different. You need a support system for your career. You need other people to help you regain your edge.
About now you are thinking, "Other people? Yeah, right. That
is exactly what I need, another way to embarrass myself further

by inviting others to share my misery." Okay, I understand that what you really want to do is crawl back into bed, pull the covers over your head, and go back to sleep until you wake up tomorrow and realize that this has all been a really bad dream.

We are at an important juncture in your comeback. The next critical step involves finding out who you can lean on for emotional support, practical advice, and opportunities.

Your needs will change from day to day as you move further along in your comeback. Yet one thing will remain constant: you can't do it alone. You need other people. Consistently, the people who are the most resilient and most successful at coming back from a career setback are those with a strong external support network and an equally strong framework of internal faith and belief.

Your support system is a combination of *external* and *internal* support and consists of three key elements:

◇ Other people
◇ Groups
◇ Yourself

In the beginning of life, when we are infants, we need others to survive, right? And at the end of life, you need others to survive, right? But here is the secret: In between, we need others as well. —*Mitch Albom*, Tuesdays with Morrie

What Type of Support Do You Need?

As you go through this experience you will need much more than job leads and a shoulder to cry on. Each of us needs support in different ways and at different times throughout our journey. As you assemble your support system consider adding people, groups, and activities that can offer the following types of support:

◇ Professional and industry-related support
◇ Job search and career strategy support
◇ Intellectual support and stimulation
◇ Family support
◇ Spiritual support
◇ An outlet for venting or complaining and letting it all out (but not your family)
◇ A source of encouragement, or a "rah-rah" cheer-leader
◇ Someone to share good news with
◇ A objective butt kicker who will "tell it like it is"
◇ Your own space—a place or activity you can es-cape to
◇ A person or group of people who are experiencing the same thing and can identify with you
◇ A place and a way to belong to something

Creating Your External Support System

Finding Support from Other People

People Want to Help You . . . If You Let Them

The people around you can help cushion the fall, help you bounce back, and ultimately help you land on your feet. But you have to take the first step and let them help you. A career setback is something that you never wish upon anyone. Your family, friends, or acquaintances likely want to help you; it is just that in many cases they either (a) aren't aware that you need help, or (b) don't know how they can help you. This is particularly true when you isolate yourself or put on a facade that "Everything is fine. I'm in control."

Whether it is your family, your close friends, a social acquaintance or professional contact or the random person you meet along the way, they can all play an important role in your support system—if you let them. Here are a few things to remember when putting together your external support system

Don't Assume People Know What You Really Do

If you want your friends to help you, help them understand what it is that you really do for a living. Think about it. How well do you really know what your friends do for a living? I'm not talking about your professional contacts, who may have a pretty good idea because you are in the same field. What about your social circle of friends?

Your friends and acquaintances may know many things about you, such as that you are allergic to shellfish and love Thai food, but they may not have a clue about what you do for a living, other than "Uh, something in real estate, I think."

Even if they have a clearer picture, it can still be inaccurate or incomplete. "He is in sales." Okay, what kind? Is he a rep, manager, VP? What industry? See my point? You may know an attorney or a doctor, but do you know what they specialize in? You may know an insurance agent, but do you know what areas she represents? The point is that often we really don't know. If this is the case, how can someone help refer you or provide a lead on a job? Make sure that your friends and contacts clearly understand what you do and what you are looking for.

People Aren't Mind Readers

You have to let people know what you do, what you are looking for, and how they can help. No one comes right out and says, "So I understand that you are out of work. I'll bet that you would like for me to grant you access to my Rolodex, make some introductions at companies that might have an opening that fits your qualifications (whatever those are), and give you my endorsement with that potential employer?"

Of course not. They are likely to say, "How can I help you?" You can't expect anyone, even your close friends or contacts, to read your mind or have an instant understanding of what you need and how they can help you. It is not another person's responsibility to play twenty questions or to guess what you need. Nor do your contacts have the time to pull answers and information out of you or read between the lines because you are too embarrassed to ask.

As I was shutting down my company and beginning to revisit my contacts, I was too embarrassed to actually say, "Well, my company went under and I'm looking for a new job." I would dance around the issue and hope that they would understand and save me from having to ask directly for help. Consequently some of my contacts didn't know quite how to help me. Some of my friends never thought to ask me because they assumed that I wanted to remain an entrepreneur and would instantly start another company or that I would immediately go back to consulting and speaking. They made their own incorrect assumptions.

Unless you specifically tell someone what you need from them and how they can help you, they will make their own incorrect assumptions. As a result, your contact or friend is not as effective a supporter as he or she could be, and you become angry or resentful. ("Why wouldn't Anthony help me?" or "Suzy couldn't really do anything.")

Three important things to remember:

⬦ Be direct in explaining your situation and what happened.

⬦ Know what you need and don't be afraid to ask for it.

⬦ The sooner you can communicate these things, the sooner you will start to see a positive reaction from those who can help you.

Help, I need somebody.   —*The Beatles*

COMEBACK EXERCISE
Tell Me About It

I know that asking for help or explaining a setback is extremely difficult. You never really become comfortable with it, but a good way to start is to practice saying it aloud to yourself. Say it in front of the mirror as you are getting ready for bed or while you are at a stoplight or in the shower. Work on the language. Hit the high points and get to the end result. Skip the narrative. If someone wants details, they will ask or you can tell them later.

If you are bitter, angry, or hurt, that's acceptable, but don't let that color your description of your situation. You can say briefly that you were hurt, surprised, or disappointed—but don't give the play-by-play on how you were treated, call your former employer or boss the great Satan himself, and say you pity the poor souls who still work for "that man." Get to the point.

There is a second step to this exercise. Repeat it as before, except this time practice asking for specific help. The type of help is up to you. It can be whatever you need. Someone to read and critique your résumé, provide a contact at certain companies, recommend a recruiter, keep their ears open for any prospects or openings, or simply lend an ear or offer advice; the choice is yours.

Practice the exact phrases and be specific. If you are mumbling, speak up. If you are fidgeting, work through it. If you are looking at your shoes, try looking at yourself in the mirror.

Sound corny? Maybe. I'm not saying that you should do this in front of your kids or at dinner with friends. Make no mistake. It is uncomfortable. But until you can say what happened and ask for the help you need, you will be stuck in first gear.

We are all angels with one wing,
able to fly only when we embrace each other.

—*Anonymous*

Don't Go to the Well Too Often

Think of your contacts as a giant bank account or debit card filled with goodwill and favors. Be mindful about how many withdrawals you make. You don't want to take advantage of anyone or be a nuisance, so save your requests for when you really need a favor. And don't forget to make a deposit occasionally by asking if there is anything that you can do for them. They realize that you may not be in a position to do anything right now, but when the time is right your contact will make a withdrawal of his or her own.

If someone is kind enough to give you a contact or lead or make an introduction for you, make sure to follow up with that person to thank them and let them know how it turned out. If I give a contact or lead to someone, I want to know if it panned out or how it went for them. I want to know if the person I suggested they speak with was helpful or not. I need to know this because if the contact later wants something from me, there is a little note in the back of my head about how they treated my friend or family member.

Find a Reason to Stay in Touch

You will talk with many people throughout your comeback. They may not be able to help you at that exact moment, but if you are persistent and keep your name in front of them by staying in touch and offering progress reports, when something does turn up, they are more likely to think of you.

To build a strong support system, you can't treat people as "drive-by" contacts: you set up a meeting, dump some data on them, ask for help, and then you don't talk to them again for months. You have to keep people concerned about you by finding reasons to consistently stay in touch.

Your family and close friends—your sounding boards and the people you are accountable to—should hear from you daily or weekly. But for general contacts and acquaintances I suggest that you get in touch at least once a month. You can do every two weeks if it's someone you are comfortable with, or if there are earth-shattering developments, but generally it is a little soon. On the other hand, more than a month is too long to maintain any continuity.

The key to following up is to offer a piece of news or a development. Supply a relevant piece of information that can benefit them. "Hey, James, did you see that article in *Fortune*, let me send it to you." "I saw this on the Web about a client of yours. I'll e-mail it to you." Or you can give them an update or progress report. "James, I just wanted to thank you and let you know that I spoke with the contact you gave me. I have an interview scheduled next week." Or "I wanted to let you know that I have been talking with some folks at Dell." Keep people updated consistently and give them something of value in return. Let them see that their help, whether it's contacts or advice, is not wasted or unappreciated.

Avoid the Christmas Letter Approach

If you haven't seen someone in a while, it is tempting to give them a long story in an attempt to bring them up to speed about your situation. As fascinating as it might be, save the unabridged version for when you are not looking for a job.

You don't want to sound like one of those form letters that people send at the holidays. You don't hear from these people all year long and then in one supersized letter they attempt to play catch-up by giving you all of the intimate details of their trip to the Grand Canyon and how Aunt Eunice's psoriasis acted up outside of Scottsdale. Give them crackers, not the whole meal.

When Describing What You Do, Have a Point

Job seekers call my office and I will ask them, "What are you looking to do?" Three minutes later, the oxygen has stopped reaching my brain because they are still telling me what they used to do and about this enormous data conversion project they once led and . . . People don't find all of the details nearly as relevant or interesting as you think they do. Have a point and get to it quickly. If they want more detail or need to follow up, they will ask. Also, speak in clear terms that someone who is not intimately familiar with the field can understand. Stay away from acronyms or buzzwords and don't assume that someone knows what you are talking about.

Who You Spend Time with Determines Your Outlook and Success

When you were a kid, did your mom ever get onto you for hanging out with the "wrong crowd"? Well, I've got news for you . . . she was right. When you're coming back from a career setback, who you spend time with is critical. It can make or break you.

The people you surround yourself with will affect your thoughts, your motivation, your mood, your entire outlook. They can determine whether you have a positive outlook or whether you become mired in self-doubt and sarcasm.

Be Around People Who Know You for Something Other Than Your Career

I grew up playing competitive tennis and played in college. While I don't move quite like I did fifteen years and thirty pounds ago, I'm still pretty good. Going out to play with a group of people who knew me in a context that did not involve work was tremendously helpful during my comeback. For one thing, I was out of the house. And I was around people who didn't evaluate me based on my profession. They thought, "He has a good backhand and is fun to play doubles with." It was a small way for me to feel good about myself.

Be Around People Who Are Working

Job support groups are great, but ultimately you need to spend a significant portion of your time with people who are employed. The first reason is that they are more likely to make introductions and help you find a job than your unemployed friends are. And second there is a different energy and enthusiasm that surrounds people who are working than there is surrounding groups of people who are not. There is a sense of urgency, but not desperation.

Be Around People Who Are Positive, Energetic, and Optimistic

Place yourself around as many happy, upbeat optimists as you can find. You need to view the glass as half full during this time. There will be inevitable disappointments, so if you are around positive energy, it is harder for you to stay down. Don't know any adults like this? Spend time with a small child. Seriously. Nothing will lift your spirits, give you a laugh, and help you keep things in perspective like talking and playing with a little kid.

Misery Loves Company

During my comeback, it turned out that many of my professional contacts were in the same boat as I was, shaking their heads, wondering how to pick up the pieces of their careers and reposition themselves. Several of us commiserated daily via e-mail and phone, lamenting our current employment situation, or lack of one. But after a while the gallows humor became too much for me to deal with. The tone was cynical and unproductive. It is easy to fall into this trap. Be careful who you spend time with. You need an outlet where you can vent to people who understand what you are going through, but when it becomes consistently negative, you need to break away.

Be Accountable to Someone

One of the critical members to add to your support system is someone whom you can be accountable to. Choose a close friend, a former coworker who has undergone a similar challenge, a professional career coach or counselor, a professional colleague or mentor. Who it is doesn't matter as long as they can shoot straight with you. This should be a person who will push you, make you do the things that you don't want to do but that are necessary in finding a job, someone who isn't afraid to ask you, "Did you write your follow-up notes?" and with whom you can go over your schedule and progress. You need a person who can tell you bluntly to "stop talking about it and do it" when you overanalyze whether to call a prospect.

I know this sounds like a huge commitment. You aren't looking for a baby-sitter, but someone who will challenge you. The best person for this task is someone who is going through a similar experience. That way you can return the favor and they will know exactly what you are going through. Make sure that they are at about the same experience level as you. You need someone who can act as a contemporary. If you were part of a downsizing or layoff, a former coworker is a good choice. Ask if you can meet or talk regularly and help each other out as you go through your job search and comeback. If you don't have a former coworker or friend who is also going through a comeback, you can try meeting someone through a career support group or your outplacement office if you have one, or even call on a close friend whom you can count on. This person's role is similar to that of an athletic trainer or workout partner. If you have worked out with a training partner before, you know that they will push you when you aren't trying hard enough, encourage you when necessary, help you with your form, give you tips, tell you objectively when you are getting off track, cheer you on when you make progress, and lay some heavy guilt on you when you sleep in, whine, or wimp out.

I strongly discourage you from choosing your spouse, partner, or even parent to take on this role. You are naturally going to feel accountable to them anyway. However, there is already some natural tension built into the situation, and they are simply too close to be objective. It becomes easy to mistake constructive criticism for nagging. It can also disrupt the balance of power in the relationship and cause additional stress that neither of you need. There is too much baggage there. Choose someone who is unconnected to the situation and who isn't directly affected by the outcome.

Finding Support from Networking and Support Groups

Job seekers and career changers at all levels commonly turn to the many job search, support, and networking groups available for support, encouragement, and information. Generally these career- or job search–oriented groups have a dedicated focus to either support and development or networking and lead generation. Such groups can be as dramatically different and diverse as the populations they serve.

Job- and Career-Oriented Groups

Job Support or Career Development Groups. The primary objective of these groups is to assist people with career development or job search skills. They provide advice and support by letting you network and communicate with others in similar situations. Some of these people may be currently employed and are looking to enhance their careers or prepare to make a move, while the majority may be "in between" jobs or actively looking. These groups may provide networking for job leads as a minor element, but they are mainly educational and supportive.

Job Search Networking Groups. While these groups may offer advice or have speakers, the emphasis is on sharing and discovering job leads and openings.

Both types of groups may have an established structure for each meeting. It may take the form of a classroom or seminar setting, a roundtable discussion, or a reception or mixer followed by a main presentation. Some follow a set curriculum over several weeks with course materials, books, exercises, and a theme or topic for each meeting.

Most career- or job-related groups are local or regional in nature. They go by names such as the Five-o-clock Club in New York City (www.fiveoclockclub.com), Professionals in Transition (PIT) (www.jobsearching.org) in North Carolina, and 40 Plus of Philadelphia (www.40plus.org). These groups also have chapters in other cities.

There is also a handful of national career networking groups. One of the most popular is Exec-u-net. It is a fee-based group geared for people at the managerial and executive level. They hold monthly meetings around the country and offer services on their website. To learn more visit www.execunet.com.

If you want to learn about job search, support, and career

development groups in your area, contact your local workforce commission or employment office or look in your local newspaper's business section or your local business journal or magazine. You can check out www.careercomeback.com for a comprehensive listing of groups and meetings, including links.

Two other great places to locate these types of groups or meetings are www.careerjournal.com, which offers a free state-by-state listing of local career and job search meetings, and the Riley Guide (www.rileyguide.com).

Does It Cost Me Anything to Join a Career or Job Search Group?

Most are free. They are generally open to the community and usually have very few restrictions. If there are charges, it is usually a nominal fee to cover materials or lunch. A few of the national or executive-level groups may charge a meeting or member fee, but most groups cost nothing to attend.

Who Sponsors the Groups?

Most job search or career-oriented groups are sponsored by civic or religious organizations, the local government, or community, employer, or industry consortiums or alumni groups, even private organizations.

Don't get hung up on who sponsors the group as much as what the group offers and who it caters to. The main things you should be concerned with are who attends the group and what the level of discussion is. Diversity is great, but you want to lean toward groups that meet the needs of people with your experience level or who are in your industry.

For example, many of the government-sponsored groups tend to attract people in blue-collar, low-level service positions without a college education. The religious-sponsored groups tend to draw a larger crowd of educated professionals from a broad selection of experience levels and industries. Industry groups lean toward a particular discipline, such as technology or finance, and may tend to attract people at a certain experience level, depending on the group.

Find One That Works for You

As with anything, there are good groups and there are bad ones. Some are dynamic and proactive, and others have all the excitement of bingo night at Golden Acres. Find a group that meets your needs and personality. A group is only as good as the facilitator or leader and the participants. Go for the people, the agenda, and the leader. Not every group will meet your needs. Try different ones. You will also outgrow some as you reach different stages in your comeback. If a group isn't meeting your needs, find another one. Your time is too precious.

While every group is different, the general support and networking groups tend to attract an older, more experienced audience. Twenty- and thirtysomethings are noticeably absent from many of the general groups. They tend to gravitate to industry organizations or events and groups that may include a social element. Go where you are comfortable, and with what is right for you.

The size of the meeting doesn't matter. It all depends on what you are comfortable with. Be prepared for a lot of turnover, as groups tend to change frequently as members come and go. This is particularly true in career support and job search groups. When people find jobs, they often have little need for the group anymore, so they stop coming. Be prepared for your group to have an ebb and flow, and when it stops meeting your needs, don't bemoan the fact that it isn't like it used to be . . . just move on to another one.

Be Clear About What You Need

Know what you want from the group and what its objective is. Do you need it as a morale booster, for job tips, leads, camaraderie? As you start evaluating groups, contact the facilitator, leader, or coordinator to ask what the group covers and find out about its focus and makeup. Be sure to ask if the group's emphasis is more on job leads and networking or on job search strategy and support.

Many people attend a group expecting to swap job leads or learn of openings, then quickly grow frustrated when they learn that it is a support group. Most have elements of each but generally lean one way or the other.

If you feel that you need additional help beyond a group or if the group is not going in a direction you would like, talk to the facilitator or director. You might let her know what you need. People at different levels attend, and it is difficult to meet everyone's needs. If you need more, ask for a one-on-one session. If you get no response, change groups.

Know Who Dispenses the Advice

With a support or strategy group, ask where the bulk of the information comes from. Is it from a facilitator or counselor? Is it a local outplacement expert or coach? Is it a local human resources executive or recruiter? Do they bring in guest speakers and professionals? Do they follow a guide, text, or particular strategy? Does the advice come from group participants who relay experiences that have recently worked for them? All of these are fine. But know who the leader is, why they are leading, and what the plan is. I'm not a regimented black-and-white type of guy, but I believe that a group such as this should have a purpose, agenda, and plan. Otherwise it is just a gathering of people. Your time is too valuable for that.

Stay away from groups where the inmates run the asylum. You will be able to tell quickly if a group has any outspoken "groupies" or "regulars." This is not a good sign. They are usually the most vocal, most opinionated people and have an idea or comment on everything you should do. They also have probably been unemployed the longest and have no success rate to base any of their sage advice on. Their lives revolve around these meetings. Every group has at least one person like this . . . but if you notice an abundance of these people or if one person is consistently allowed to steal the show and rob everyone else of their time, move on. The leader has lost control and you will be miserable.

Groups Offer a Community of People Who Understand What You Are Going Through

One of the benefits of participating in a group is that it can temporarily replace the community that existed in your previous job. It gives you a destination and something to look forward to amid possible isolation and rejection. These groups can help people work through the emotions of anger, sadness, and bitterness and lead them ultimately to healing. It is helpful to talk with other people who completely understand what you are going through. It can ease the isolation and give you a sense of belonging and normalcy. It can be a positive way for you to feel like a contributor again.

Be Strategic About Who You Sit With

If you go to a group event with another person, it is easy to stick together like kids at a junior high dance, hugging the wall and afraid to leave the safety of the group you know. As uncomfortable as it may be to attend a group meeting or event, when you do go, try to get out of your comfort zone and sit with new people. (Your friend may be great, but he isn't going to help you get a job.) You may already know some people there, but sitting with strangers each time will give you greater exposure and expand your contacts.

Also, be strategic about who you sit with. For example, if you are attending a professional group meeting or luncheon that has open seating, subtly look at the name tags of the people sitting around the table before you choose where to sit. If there is someone representing a particular company that you are interested in, pull up a chair. If you see a table filled with people from many different companies, again pull up a chair. But if it appears that everyone at the table is with the same group, you might move on. Sit where you can maximize your time and effort and meet as many people as possible.

Can I Get a Job Through These Groups?
Are They Worth It?

Are they worth it? Well, that is a tough one. I'll give you a definite . . . maybe. It really depends on what you consider to be a successful result for you. If to you success means learning some additional skills and tips, finding people you can talk to who understand what you are going through, discovering resources you can use, or having a place to go where you can experience some camaraderie, then yes, you will likely be successful. However, if you are looking to find a job as a direct result of attending a meeting or group, I'd say that the chances are pretty slim. It depends on the individual group, and while it can happen, I wouldn't go to Las Vegas and bet the milk money on it.

These groups are best at providing you with support and skills that can ultimately help you to land a job, but their strength is not in placing people, nor is it really their primary objective. People generally benefit more from the camaraderie and advice than they do from the job leads and openings. Industry groups are the exception to this, because of your close proximity to employers.

It is a common misconception among job seekers that whether it's a group, a recruiter, or a website, all you have to do is show up or put your name out there and the system will take care of things for you. That is just wrong. If you know this going in, you can operate more quickly and effectively, because you won't be bogged down hoping for something that simply isn't there.

Don't Become a Support Group Junkie

If you aren't careful you can make a full-time job out of attending job search and support groups. They are very helpful, but don't make them your main priority. There are so many groups out there that you could spend the bulk of your time attending meetings about how to find a job rather than actually going out and getting one. Don't be like the athlete who always practices but freaks out when it is time to get in the game. Be stingy with your time and don't use the groups as a crutch or an excuse for not doing what it takes to actually find a job. Remember what the real goal is.

Business Networking and Lead Groups

Groups of this type are often business oriented and are not focused on the job seeker, but rather are used to generate referrals and leads for business opportunities. Sometimes referred to as lead groups, these networking groups are often made up of business owners, independent professionals like lawyers or insurance agents, salespeople, and others who are looking to generate business through referrals.

Different from traditional job search groups, these are probably the least successful of all groups for job seekers, although more and more job seekers are attending them, with mixed results. These groups are geared to generate new business, referrals, and sales, not to help job seekers. Everyone here is looking for business. And if you are unemployed, sorry, but you are not the most desirable person in the room to talk to. People are there asking, "What can this person do for me?" Sure, their companies might be looking for employees, but that is not why they come to these meetings.

Your task is to be a giver. Present yourself as an industry expert who can help them understand your business and offer your expertise, knowledge, and insight into a certain field or the market. When you are back on your feet you will be in a position to buy from them and return the favors. If you understand this, you won't be as disappointed when attending a networking meeting.

Each networking group has a different makeup and feel, so

it is important that you find one that not only feels right for you, but offers the type of people and contacts that you need. I've been to some groups whose members were jewelers, plumbers, attorneys, insurance salesmen, and landscapers. Great. You may be in the market for all of their services some-day, but these are not exactly the types of contacts you need to be making if you want a job in human resources or advertising. Go where those people gather. Call the director or leader and ask what type of people attend and what professions are rep-resented. You can usually find a listing of these groups in your local paper or business publication. If your local paper does not list them, you should check out your local library.

Religious Organizations and Groups

Many churches, temples, and other religious organizations of-fer support groups or classes for area job seekers. These can be networking, support, or strategy meetings. While they are sometimes for members only, most are open to the general public, regardless of your personal religious affiliation. In fact many job seekers attend a variety of groups across all denomi-nations. In Dallas job seekers tend to travel a little triangle, hit-ting the major job groups provided by the Presbyterian Church, the Baptist Church, and the Jewish Family Service. All are welcome. Don't worry or let a group's religious affiliation intimidate you. There is actually very little, if any, proselytizing at these meetings. If your local church or temple doesn't offer a group, contact the local or regional office of your particular denomination to see if another organization offers meetings. For example, in most major cities the Jewish Family Service of-fers monthly support groups and services for the community that are often open to everyone.

Corporate Alumni Programs

If you worked for a large company, find out if they have an alumni group or website established for former employees. This is a trend that has recently grown in popularity. The group may be a formal initiative authorized by the company or it may be a labor of love that is overseen by former coworkers. Some offer a way for former colleagues to stay in touch with one another or offer assistance with benefits, severance issues, insurance, or job leads. Some, like the former employees' group of Nortel, have aligned themselves with an outplacement firm to offer career services to their colleagues. And some are set up as a forum to vent, gripe, and moan about the company or former managers. Some of these groups allow companies to post job openings on the alumni site. Why do companies do this? Katie Weiser, global director of alumni relations at Deloitte Consulting, says, "Our people will be movers and shakers wherever they land. We're planting seeds for the future." Check with your former employer's human resources department or go on the Web and do a Google or Yahoo search for "[your company name] alumni" or "[company name] ex-employees."

Professional Associations and Industry Groups

If you still belong to a professional group or trade association, this can be not only a great source of support, but one of your best resources for quickly landing another gig in your field.

Associations exist primarily to facilitate business and promote the profession. One way that they do this is through educational and professional development. It is in the profession's best interest to help people develop their skills and to have their membership successfully employed.

There has been a growing trend within associations and professional groups to offer coaching, seminars, counseling, and job search advice and services. Some have even developed elaborate job boards and networking opportunities that can

MEMBERSHIP HAS ITS PRIVILEGES

Even if your industry group doesn't offer formal services for job seekers, you can still accelerate your chances of finding support and a solid lead by utilizing your association membership. Here's how. Volunteer. Yep, it is that simple. You should call up your local or regional chapter (if you can't locate one, call the national office) and start by contacting one of the officers or a board member. The board members and officers are usually listed in the newsletter, in other publications, or on the website. Calling the president is not a bad place to start. Say that you are a member and that you would really like to become more involved by joining a committee. (By the way, you should also start attending the meetings regularly.)

These groups are always in need of volunteers and will welcome your offer—even if it is somewhat self-serving. Here is what is in it for you (other than a great way to get involved and contribute). First of all you will be surrounded by people (always a good thing), but more important you will be surrounded by people who are working, and working in your field, no less. These people are dialed in and networked to what is going on around town. They know who is hiring and who is not and they know who match employers with their members. To borrow from the old American Express tag line, "Membership has its privileges."

Contact your association. Make sure to explore both your national organization and its local or regional chapter. Ask to speak with someone in membership services or on the educational and professional development committee. Also check

the players, movers and shakers, and contacts are. This is a gold mine. You may have been trying to get in with a particular company for weeks and suddenly you find yourself working side by side on a committee with its head. It is a wonderful, unassuming way to stay current in the field, contribute, and make valuable contacts.

One other tip: if you have a choice of committees, I suggest that you check out the membership committee. This is an extremely visible group that has access to many people among both current and new members. What a wonderful opportunity for you to get your name out there and to see who the players are. It also allows you to contact people in a nonthreatening and legitimate way . . . and if the conversation later happens to turn to "what do you do?" you then have a great opportunity to sell yourself. Other good committees for visibility include programming, meetings, and publicity. But in the end go where you are comfortable and feel that you can make a valuable contribution. This will keep you involved and contributing, but more important it will keep you working side by side with and in front of people in the industry who can hire you. By the way, no one will turn you down because you currently aren't working. Go for it.

PAYING YOUR DUES

Remember when I said in the opening chapter that you should renew your memberships when things start to look bleak at your company? Here is why. Now that you are without a job, you certainly don't want to pony up several hundred bucks to renew your membership. Still, don't worry if you didn't renew: ask your association if they have "hardship" dues, reduced fees, or special arrangements for members who have lost their job. Most will work with you.

---

out the association's website to see what resources it offers. Many groups have sections on their website that allow you to post your résumé or offer job listings. Visit the American Society of Association Executives (www.asaenet.org) for a directory of professional and trade groups in the United States.

Stay in the Loop Professionally

Just because you aren't working in your field doesn't mean that you shouldn't stay involved. Staying in touch with your professional colleagues and with the current happenings in your industry is one of the most effective ways to land another job. Here are several ways to stay in the loop.

Offer to Present at Meetings

Use your professional and industry expertise to gain exposure. Many groups invite speakers and professionals in their field to present at monthly meetings or gatherings. Offer your services. Contact the person who heads up the meetings or programs committee and offer to speak on an industry-related subject or perhaps sit on a panel.

Attend Meetings and Industry Gatherings

Attend as many industry-related or professional meetings as you can. While career support and search groups fill a certain void, professional meetings and groups are more likely to produce a solid job lead than anything else. The information you get from these groups can help you to stay current in your industry and make you visible to the decision makers.

Register for All of the Boards and Newsletters

There are a variety of online message boards and newsgroups dedicated to each profession or industry. Most are free and offer a daily e-mail newsletter or synopsis of the discussion boards. Register for as many of these as possible. Participate in the discussions and offer your thoughts when applicable. It is a great way to stay in touch with others in the field, and can be a great source for leads as well.

Read Up on Your Industry or Profession

Just because you lost your job, you shouldn't stop caring about what goes on in your profession. Things change so quickly that unless you are staying current and reading about deals, recent developments, movements, and trends, how can you expect to speak intelligently about the industry when you aren't working in it every day?

Subscribe to the e-mail newsletters and monitor the bulletin boards and discussion groups for your industry. Read the trade journals and publications for your field. Remember when I said to renew your subscriptions before you left the company? This is why. If you don't have them or can't afford them, check out the publication's website or go to your library. You might even ask a former coworker to float you a copy.

Creating Your Internal Support System

Your family, your friends, or even a networking or support group can give you advice and help keep you on track, but when it comes down to it, no one else can save you. You have to save yourself. When times are tough and your external support system isn't able to give you what you need, your only choice is to look inside and rely on your own abilities and faith to get you through to the next step.

Keep Your Mind and Body Sharp

> **Iron rusts from disuse; stagnant water loses its purity and in cold weather becomes frozen; even so does inaction sap the vigor of the mind.** —*Leonardo da Vinci*

In the early 1980s movie *Mr. Mom*, Michael Keaton portrays an automobile designer who loses his job in a big corporate layoff. Unable to find work, he decides to stay at home and care for his three small children while his wife pursues her career in advertising. Keaton continues to search for work, but finding it difficult he starts to give up both mentally and physically, gaining weight, failing to shave, and wearing the same flannel shirt day after day. But the funniest (if not the most accurate) portrayal shows him talking to the television and enjoying the same show as his one-year-old daughter until he finally screams, *"My mind is mush. I'm watching* Sesame Street *with the kids, and I'm liking it."*

Sound familiar? Okay, maybe you are changing clothes more than once a week, and children's programs might not be making you crazy (although the Wiggles can drive most anyone to the brink), but you still need an internal support system to keep your mind and your body sharp.

It is extremely easy to let your mind and body waste away from inactivity, despair, or distraction. The irony is that now that you have more time on your hands and are able to take care of yourself, you don't.

Have a Place to Escape To

After hours of surfing the Web in search of leads or after making call after call, you need not only a break, but a change of scenery. The pressure, rejection, and boredom can get to be too much.

Find a place or an activity that allows you to get away from everything, recharge your batteries, and clear your mind, if only for a few moments. This should be your little sanctuary. It can be a route that you run or walk in the neighborhood. It can be a drive through the country or suburbs. Several times I got in the car and drove from Dallas all the way to the Oklahoma border, ninety miles away, just to think in a different environment. Your escape can be a destination like a restaurant, the library, a park, a gym, or even a Starbucks. Quiet is good, but not required.

Oddly enough, it seems that some Starbucks have gone from being the meeting place of entrepreneurs sipping lattes as they pitched business plans and discussed stock options, to becoming the new gathering place of the unemployed. On any morning you can see the pairs gathered in impromptu networking meetings or informal interviews, and discussions of experience and résumés have become the norm. Where you go or what you do to get away from the nuts and bolts of your job search doesn't matter as much as the fact that you go to a different place. It is easier to think differently in a different environment.

It is tough to think of a solution or determine your next move when you are being bombarded by your own destructive thoughts or by people asking, "How is the search going?" Create an environment where you can be alone with your thoughts. Listen to soothing music without any lyrics. I'm not saying that you have to start chanting and drinking herbal tea, but find a way to get out of your head and away from distractions and external noise so you can really think about where you are and where you want to go.

Get Back on a Schedule and Develop a System

One of the toughest parts of dealing with a career setback is loss of the control and structure that once governed your life. Your patterns, habits, and rules have changed. It is easy to feel lost without a place to go, people to see, or a schedule. Here are four things you can do to try to replicate the structure you had while working.

Have a Schedule. Just as you got up for work every day and had a place to go and things to do, create a schedule for yourself regarding your job search. This can be as simple as getting up at a regular time, planning your calls at a certain time of day, or conducting your Web searching at a consistent time. Extend your schedule to include weekly activities, such as designating Tuesday and Thursday as your days to have lunch with a contact.

Be Around Other People. Make sure that you plan to be around people each day. You don't have to schedule meetings or interviews, but you should make it a point to get out and have some human contact at least once each day. A job search and setback can be isolating enough. Don't make it worse.

Give Yourself Little Rewards. You may have had little "carrots," or incentives, set up at work to help you get through the boring or tedious tasks. "If I get my expense report finished I will leave early today." Do the same with your search. Create little rewards for yourself when you reach certain milestones or achievements or complete a certain task. "If I send out all of my thank-you notes by noon, I'll go to Starbucks or go for a run."

Have Something You Look Forward to Each Day. Include at least one positive thing in your day that you look forward to. It can be a task or activity, or a planned conversation with one of your contacts.

All work and no play makes Jack a dull boy.

—The Shining

Get into a Workout Routine

It's not uncommon to beat yourself up about what has happened. If you let yourself go physically, start to become unkempt and disheveled or gain some weight, your self-esteem can really go through the floor.

If you already have a regular workout or fitness routine, good for you. Keep it up. It is an important release and gives you something to take your mind off your comeback . . . if only for a few hours a week. If you aren't taking care of yourself physically or have abandoned your routine, then you need to get going today. Not only will you feel and look better physically, but you will feel better mentally as well. It doesn't matter what type of activity you do. It can be something as simple as going for a walk or as structured as participating in a team sport or joining a class.

What's holding you back? "I have to focus all of my energy on my job search." "I don't have time for anything else." Really? I would think that right now you have nothing but time.

I know where you are coming from with this argument. I've used it. During my comeback I tried to fill every minute with frenetic activity. I started pulling all-nighters surfing the Web for opportunities, information, and leads (I couldn't sleep anyway). I spent my days making calls and burning up e-mail. It didn't take long for me to look and feel like an extra from *Dawn of the Dead.*

So you don't have time to keep your mind and body sharp? Let's look at this realistically. If you are unemployed, it is highly unlikely that you are spending eight to ten uninterrupted, effective quality hours on your job search, plus evenings. And if you really are spending that much time interviewing and "networking" and haven't lined anything up yet, then you obviously aren't doing something right. The key is not going to be working longer or more intensely. It is going to be taking a step back and blocking out an hour a day for yourself so you don't run out of gas. If you fall apart, everything else falls apart. Here are a few other ways to refill your tank.

After Michael was let go from his second company in two years, he began running. He was never a runner and has always been a little heavy as an adult, but the daily running was an escape. "It became my time alone with my thoughts, away from the wife, the baby, the reminder that people depended on me." It was also an exhaust valve from the frustrations that come with a job search. "The more frustrated I was the harder I ran." But there was another incredible benefit. In the course of three months during Michael's comeback he lost over twenty pounds. He had more energy, was healthier, and looked much better than he ever did when he was working fifty-plus hours a week. You don't need an expensive gym or a lot of money. Running is the perfect sport if you are unemployed . . . all you need are shorts and shoes.

Take a Class

Another way to keep your mind sharp is to take a class or learn something new. What you study is entirely up to you. You may want to take a course that will help you update or acquire a skill that makes you more marketable. But you can also look into something completely unrelated to your former everyday life, even something that seems frivolous. Check out your local community college or community center. They are always offering inexpensive courses in a variety of subjects. Even if it is a half-hour seminar or a one-night cooking class, find something that uses your mind and pushes your boundaries.

Offer Your Services in the Community

When you cease to make a contribution, you begin to die.
—*Eleanor Roosevelt*

Serving your community gives you a sense of belonging and contribution while allowing you to network. You can do a variety of things, whether it is volunteering for a local agency or offering your services to an organization that is close to your heart, like your child's school or your local church or temple. For example, if your experience is as an accountant, why don't you volunteer your time helping an organization out with their bookkeeping? It helps others and allows you to use your mind and be challenged.

Faith + Action = Results

The size of your success is determined by the size of your belief. —*Lucius Annaeus Seneca*

It doesn't matter what religion or faith you subscribe to. You can be Christian, Jewish, Muslim, Buddhist. You can worship trees or you can belong to the Main Street Church of the Frog People for all I care. You don't have to be "religious" or even "spiritual" to be successful in your comeback, but you do have to have faith.

Faith plays an enormous role in determining how you approach and cope with the challenges you will face. Faith means different things to everyone. To some faith takes on a religious meaning. You may have faith that something larger than yourself is guiding you and has a bigger plan in mind for you. Others take comfort in the faith that they will be given strength to make it through this and that good things are waiting for them around the corner. And yet others have faith in themselves and their abilities. Regardless of how you define faith or what it means to you, having faith is critical to your internal support system.

Before you conclude that this is just my opinion or that it is some way for me to sneak a message in here, hold on. I'm not promoting one flavor or another or pushing anything on you. I've made my choice and I'm keeping it to myself for now. But when I started interviewing people for this book and working with job seekers during the recent economic downturn, an interesting thing happened. There were three words that consistently turned up in almost every conversation: *community*, *contribution*, and *faith*. It didn't matter if someone was deeply religious or not, almost everyone, down to the last person, cited faith as having an enormous role in how they coped with the challenges they faced throughout their comeback. Comments like this were heard from people of all religions and degrees of faith. Some were incredibly spiritual people, others had not practiced for years, yet each said that faith and belief is what kept them going every day or when things looked their darkest.

Faith is important but it is only part of the equation. You can have faith that things will get better for you or that you will be presented with an opportunity, but you have to take the first step. Faith without action is useless. Faith plus action is a powerful combination that makes incredible things start to happen.

Tens of millions of people are familiar with the biblical story of Moses parting the Red Sea, allowing the Jewish people to escape from Egypt as Pharaoh's army chased them. Many people believe that Moses (or Charlton Heston) simply raised his staff, prayed, and the seas opened up. But that is only partially correct. Moses's faith got things ready, but it was a little-

> ## "I Know We Haven't Talked in a While, but I Need a Favor"
>
> You may never pray at all unless you are in a real bind and only then when things are at their darkest. "O God, please get me out of this and I promise I will never ask you for anything ever again . . . until the next time."
>
> A setback of this nature can be an enormous wake-up call. It can show you that you might not be in control of your life as you had previously believed. As painful as this lesson is, it is a valuable one.

known Jewish slave who put everything into motion. According to Rabbi Robert Hass, Moses was praying for God to deliver his people as the soldiers bore down on them. Their only choice was to face the soldiers or head into the sea. Everyone was scared, knowing that they would surely die in the sea, but it wasn't until one of the men, hearing Moses's prayers, had faith enough to begin walking into the sea. Only then did the waters begin to part. Believing isn't enough. You have to believe and take the steps in the right direction.

> Synchronicity—a meaningful coincidence of two or more events, where something other than the probability of chance is involved.
> —Carl Jung

CAREER COMEBACK FUNDAMENTALS
Finding Your Support System

◇ People aren't mind readers. They can't help you unless you let them know that you need help and want it.

◇ Don't assume people know exactly what you do or want to do.

◇ Visit a variety of job search or career networking groups. Look to professional groups, religious organizations, and local business groups as a resource. They are all different, so find one that works for you.

◇ Don't become too dependent on the groups. They can become your job if you aren't careful.

◇ Who you spend time with determines your outlook. Maintain contact with a diverse group of people. Include people who are going through the same thing you are, people who are working, and people who are energetic and enthusiastic.

◇ Misery loves company. Avoid spending too much time with people who are only focused on what is wrong with their comeback.

◇ Have faith in something. Believe that things will get better but act to make it happen.

Find Out What Matters to You

In the time of your life, live.
—William Saroyan

Making a career comeback means more than simply getting another job. It means making your next move, the *right move* at this particular stage in your life. Getting another job (any job) may go a long way toward helping you restore your confidence and get back on your feet, but what if you want more than "just another job"?

What if your ego and identity were wrapped up in your career and now you feel lost without your title or professional identity to cling to? What if you want your next move to make a difference or have meaning? What if you want your next move to give you control over your life, so you can devote more time and energy to your family or personal interests? What if you have always been a winner and now fear that a stigma will follow you?

Everyone's comeback is different, but what is consistent is that a comeback forces you to summon your courage and examine what matters to you, which is critical in making your next move the right one. The next important step is about helping you to find your confidence and identity and discover what is important in your life so you can choose your next move wisely.

As crazy as it seems, this is an opportunity to really look at your life in an unfiltered way, when you aren't operating on autopilot, with deadlines, projects, and political agendas to deal with. This is a time when you can be introspective and find out what matters and is important to you.

Remember Who You Are

You Haven't Changed . . . Just Your Title Has

Po Bronson, author of *What Should I Do with My Life?* calls it "The Cocktail Party Question." "So what do you do for a living?" That simple question can paralyze a normally confident and accomplished adult and reduce him to a stammering idiot. "Uh, I'm between jobs." Or "Well, I used to be . . . " or "In my former life I was . . . "

Regardless of how you arrived at your current state, whether it was your fault or not, your public label, title, or persona has changed. Not being able to lean on your career or profession can be frightening if you have long relied on a title, position, or company name to define yourself or shape your public image.

But while your "professional role" has changed, have *you* really changed? Outside of the obvious financial changes and the blow your ego may have taken, how have you changed? Are you a different person?

> "I know that I have accomplished things. But I have to fight my own negative thinking to remember that I have made progress in my career and remind myself that this wasn't all my fault." —Annie F.

What happens when you no longer have the prestigious title or company name to drop? What happens when you are known for years as Jim or Jane with WXY Company, and suddenly you are just Jim or Jane? Many who lack an identity outside of work cling to the past, much like the high school cheerleader or homecoming king, who at age 35 realizes that he or she peaked during senior year and life has been downhill ever since.

This is manifested by an overdependence on describing yourself in the past tense. For example, "I used to be . . . " "For over twenty years I was . . . " or "I'm the former . . . " Great, but what are you now? And more important, *who* are you now?

When you were asked to give up your garage key and parking pass, did your employer also ask you to leave behind your experience, skills, talents, contacts, decision-making ability, track record, accomplishments, professionalism, communication skills, ethics, or creativity? Of course not. You still have those things. Nothing about you has changed, except for the fact that you are now on the market and available. You are a free agent. You are the same person you were before, only now you have a new direction and new choices to make.

> "I loved working for Accenture and was proud of it. But now that I'm gone it doesn't change who I am or my abilities." —Shelly W.

Your true identity is not a singular one, but rather multiple identities based on the roles you play at a given time and in a given situation. You have an identity as an employee or professional, but you also have an identity as a parent, child, friend, spouse, brother or sister, community member, athlete, volunteer, or teammate. The importance of each role you play is constantly changing and depends on what you are going through at that moment. As each situation demands, one role gives way to another.

If one role presents a challenge or is altered (your career in this case), then leaning on the other roles and areas in your life (friendships, family, hobbies, faith, and community involvement or outside interest) can support and buoy your confidence. One role is temporarily diminished while another moves into its place. Rotating the roles you play, rather than relying on your professional title or occupation to determine your identity, can make a career setback less of a shock to the system.

True self-confidence and a positive professional self-image come from the sum of your experiences, beliefs, values, and abilities, not from a title or from being associated with a certain company. Titles can be empty and companies can go out of business or lose their luster. Think about it. People once took great pride in saying they worked for Enron or Arthur Andersen.

Today it is estimated that the average person will have approximately eleven different jobs, in five or six careers, throughout his or her lifetime. Some of those changes will be

> "Just because I'm unemployed doesn't mean that I don't have value. Every job I've gotten is better than the one before, and my former employers are using my work. I'm validated." —Jaime S.

by choice, others by force or circumstance. It is not a question of "What if things change?" Things *will* change. It is inevitable, and you can't let your whole life and identity be ripped apart when they do. Your career is a crucial part of your life, but it is only one part of the total package. Work is what you do; it doesn't define who you are.

This Is a Temporary Situation

As of this writing, it is estimated that it takes approximately four months to find a job, the longest time in seventeen years. Whether your comeback takes four weeks, four months, or longer, it can feel like you will be knocked down forever.

One of the hardest things to do is remind yourself that this is temporary. In the grand scheme of things, this is a snapshot, a picture of one brief period in time.

The waiting, delays, and anxiety can cause your self-esteem and confidence to drop. As time drags on, it becomes easy to think that this will stick with you for the rest of your career. But you couldn't be more wrong.

This is not the defining moment or event of your life. It is not how you will be remembered or viewed for eternity. The truth is, while it may be etched in your memory forever, down the road it won't matter to anyone else.

Let's look at a few high-profile examples to illustrate my point about career setbacks being temporary.

◇   Whether you love him or hate him, when you think of Rush Limbaugh, do you think of a successful broadcaster or someone who has been fired seven times?

◇   When you think of Lee Iacocca, do you think of one of the first truly high-profile CEOs, the man who created the

Mustang and who led the Chrysler Corporation out of bankruptcy, or do you think of someone who was fired from Ford Motor Company?

◇ Take the author J. K. Rowling. Do you think of her as the author and creator of Harry Potter, the most successful children's literary franchise in history and recently named Britain's wealthiest woman? Or do you think of her as the unemployed single mother writing stories in longhand as she sat in cafés and on trains in England eight years earlier?

These are extreme examples of people who encountered a setback, got back up on their feet, and came back stronger than ever, but how do they apply to you and your career? Simple. These famous failures were temporary.

Cynics may say, "Well, these people are famous or have plenty of money." But in fact these people were not significant household names or multimillionaires when they faced their challenges. They didn't let a temporary setback mar the remainder of their lives. They picked themselves up, found their next move, and made a significant career comeback. And the beauty of it is, while you may not ever become a broadcaster, a CEO, or an author—you can make a career comeback too.

Most of us can expect our careers to last approximately forty years. That's a long time. If you are in your twenties, thirties, or forties, you still have plenty of runway ahead of you. If you are in your fifties or sixties, this does not mean that you are put out to pasture. You can consider a change or "second act" (to use the phrase coined by Stephen Pollan, who has authored a great book by the same title).

You may or may not reach the same income level or position again, but this doesn't negate all of your previous accomplishments and achievements and the contributions you have made over the past thirty-plus years. You have much to be proud of and thankful for.

Count Your Blessings

In a crisis, it is far easier to think about what is not working in your life than it is to think of the positive things that you are blessed with. It is human nature to let all of the little things nagging at you—the doubt, the worry, and the "shoulda, coulda, wouldas"—keep you up late at night and irritate you throughout the day.

When one area of your life is not working, it can easily overshadow the areas that are working. You become so consumed with the faulty parts of your life that you neglect to see the positives. The next thing you know you have adopted a completely fatalistic view and gone from being rational ("My company is laying people off and I'm worried about my job") to being completely irrational ("No one loves me. I have bad hair. I'm fat. I'll never work again. My family would be better off without me. I'm going to have to sell the house and live under the highway, where wild dingoes will gnaw on my skinny old bones.")

Stress from a life-changing setback can produce a domino effect where the smallest thing can get us thinking that evil forces and even the world as a whole are conspiring against us.

If the car won't start in the morning, the problems start piling up on one another, and suddenly you're thinking, "My kid has a fever, the dog peed on the rug, my daughter is getting poor grades, I cut myself shaving, I need to work out, AND I DON'T HAVE A @&*%#$ JOB!!! God, what are you doing to me?" WHOA!!! Slow down and take a deep breath. Now is the time when you really need to count your blessings.

"There is always someone in a worse situation. It has made me grateful for what I have. I remind myself of those things and then it is pretty difficult to take a 'poor me' stance." —Sarah B.

If you open your heart and mind and actually start to look for blessings and positive things to happen around you, I guarantee they will start to happen more frequently. If you are looking for the swarm of locusts and the sun to grow dark and for people to avoid you, guess what you get? When you hold a strong belief, you only see confirmation of it. This is known as confirmation bias. As a result, we start seeing bad things everywhere.

I'm not saying that counting your blessings will suddenly make your phone ring with job offers. But it acts as a remarkable counterbalance to the unproductive, apocalyptic doom-and-gloom perspective that many people in this situation adopt.

We have such high expectations and are looking for the giant sign in the sky, but in reality, small victories are the key to a successful comeback. Instead of cursing the five people who wouldn't return your call or e-mail, rejoice about the one person who did respond favorably. Look for the good in things and the good things will rise to the surface.

COMEBACK EXERCISE
Count Your Blessings

Create a "blessings" list. This is going to be an ongoing exercise for you as you add to your list over time. Go outside, sit on a bench, and get out of your normal surroundings. Go to a Starbucks or café and sit down by yourself. Clear your mind and think about how you are blessed. Nothing is too large, too small, or too insignificant. List all of the things that you have to be thankful for and that are working in your life. Below are a few examples.

◇ I'm healthy.
◇ I have an education.
◇ My parents love me.
◇ I have a car that is paid off.
◇ I have a beautiful home.
◇ I have a gorgeous, intelligent spouse/partner who loves me.
◇ I have supportive friends who don't care what I do for a living.
◇ My children run to greet me whenever I come home.
◇ My child still lets me hold him like a baby.
◇ My spouse has a good job, with insurance.
◇ I have a best friend who will listen to me and accept me unconditionally.
◇ I have great experience and know many people.
◇ I'm respected by my peers.
◇ I live in a vibrant, exciting city.
◇ I'm a good speaker.
◇ I have a nice butt.
◇ I know my neighbors and feel part of my community.
◇ I'm involved in my church/temple/mosque.

The size of your list doesn't matter. In fact, the more things you can list the better for you. As time goes by, write down the little blessings you notice each day. It can be something as simple as a break in the clouds where the sun shines through or a person holding the door for you or smiling when they give you back your change.

You may think this is either the corniest thing you have ever done or it is worthwhile and right on target. Regardless, I'm here to tell you when you are on a roller-coaster ride of rejection, confusion, or disappointment, looking at this list will get your thinking and attitude back on track. These are the things that make you smile inside when all about you is swirling.

Pride—Comeback Fuel or Comeback Killer?

As children we are taught to take pride in what we do and in ourselves. Pride in your abilities, accomplishments, education, family, country, heritage, or the organization or team you represent—it can be a powerful driving force. However, pride can be a double-edged sword. It can be a career comeback killer that holds you back and clouds your vision of what really matters. Or it can fuel the internal fire that propels you. Which pride drives you? Is yours a pride that drags you down or causes you to cling to a career choice or path that might not be the best for you and those around you? Or is yours a motivating sense of pride, satisfaction, and self-respect that will help you fight to rise above what you are facing and simply do whatever it takes?

> **The happiness of your life depends on the quality of your thoughts.**
> —*Marcus Aurelius*

"What a Lovely E-mail. You Must Be So Proud."

My work requires that I travel a lot, so I spend a good amount of time on airplanes. Like many people I hate the cramped quarters—no leg room and being shoulder to shoulder with the person in the next seat who is constantly looking at my computer or papers, pretending not to notice anything.

I've sat next to a lot of talkers in my day, but in all of the years I've been flying, not once has anyone ever leaned over to me and said, "That is a gorgeous e-mail" or "What a handsome résumé" or "That's a fine-looking proposal. You must be so proud."

Earlier this year I was flying back from New York on a Continental Airlines flight when a pilot who was catching a ride home sat down next to me. As I fired up my laptop (airplanes are where I do a lot of my writing), he noticed the picture on the screen of my three kids dressed up for Halloween. I'd just added the picture of Sammy, the toothless little witch, Skylar, the smiling astronaut, and Tyler, the fuzzy giraffe, all holding their trick-or-treat loot in front of our home. The pilot tapped me on the arm and pointed to the screen. "What a beautiful family you have, you must be very proud."

You know what? I was proud. After I thanked the pilot and we talked about our kids for a little bit, I stopped and really thought about it. I was as proud of that picture and those three little people as I was of anything I'd ever done or been associated with. And the best thing about it was knowing that it was permanent and significant.

My impact as a professional is fleeting, regardless of my success. It is not like I'm saving lives. Companies come and go, jobs come and go, memos, projects, sales, and, yes, even career books come and go, but the impact I have on those three little people is timeless. It is also farther reaching than anything else I can do, because wherever they go and whoever they encounter in their lives, their actions will be a reflection of the values, lessons, and love that my wife and I have given them. Making a difference in their lives is what matters to me.

I wish I could say that it has always been that way. Like many people, I have put my career and pride in first place and asked others to make sacrifices on my behalf. But as I experienced my career comeback, I discovered what mattered to me at this stage in my life. As a result, knowing what matters to me shapes the career and personal choices that I make.

What Matters to You?

What lies behind us and what lies before us are tiny matters compared to what lies within us.

—*Ralph Waldo Emerson*

What matters to you? What do you look forward to? Let's look beyond the obvious yet legitimate answers of the "first" and the "fifteenth," or retirement. I mean, why do you get up in the morning? What lights your fire, makes you excited, or makes you smile inside? What makes you keep pushing on when things are tough and look their darkest?

I don't ask these as big, metaphysical "Where is my place in the universe?"–type questions. I ask them because it is critical that you know your motivations and what drives your decisions before you make your next move.

Given your current situation, you're probably thinking "What matters to me?" is a pretty simple question. "How about finding another job before I lose the house, my unemployment benefits run out, or I burn through my savings? That's what matters." You are absolutely right, those things matter—a lot.

Life Has a Way of Showing You What Matters

Our lives can be so hectic, trying to juggle work, family, finances, kids, keeping a relationship together, and trying to stay healthy. If you are like most people, you are tugged in so many directions simply trying to balance life's demands that it is easy to lose sight of what is important. You stop living and simply get by.

You make yourself stressed out and crazy trying to give your best to everyone in everything you do. You make sacrifices, work hard, play the game, and put up with more junk than you deserve so that you can attain a certain quality of life. But sometimes it doesn't happen like you planned. The days, weeks, and months start to blend together and you find yourself constantly looking forward to Friday, a three-day weekend, or your two weeks of vacation as if they were lost treasure.

Your pursuit of "quality of life" can become a passionless, nondescript blur that has you always looking ahead to the time when things will be different. We say to ourselves, "Things will be better when the kids are older, the house is paid off, I get that promotion or raise, I can redecorate the house, I lose weight, I meet someone and settle down, I have more money,

I can spend more time with the kids, the economy turns around, parachute pants and eight-tracks become popular again." The list can go on and on.

The point is, you are stretched so thin in an attempt to balance everything that you can't enjoy what you have or where you are. So you long for "what might be, if only . . . " and rather than achieving quality of life, you achieve quality of nothing.

As life becomes more hectic or as you fall into a rut of the routine and mundane, you can lose sight of your original purpose or destination. You forget why it is that you make the sacrifices that you do.

Everyday roadblocks and speed bumps cause you to temporarily slow down on the highway of life. Then you are back to your old ways, speeding along with your hair on fire. Often it isn't until your life hits a major setback that you begin to acknowledge what is important.

Believe it or not, right now you have a unique window of opportunity. Your setback has essentially handed you the controls of your career and your life again. Although it may not feel like it, you are in the driver's seat. You have a chance to right the course and steer your life in a new direction that truly matters to you.

Once in a while you get shown the light in the strangest of places if you look at it right.

—Jerry Garcia, The Grateful Dead

Life constantly sends us signals that gently nudge us in a certain direction or shine a spotlight on something that deserves our attention. It may be a layoff, an illness, a new relationship, a discovery, a news article or book that we read, or a change at home or at work. Some signals are subtle, some very overt and blatant. But often these signals go unnoticed because we are so consumed running the rat race that we let the urgent, rather than the important, rule our lives.

> The trouble with the rat race is that even if you win, you are still a rat.
> —*Lily Tomlin*

What Is Ruling Your Life?

"Unemployment or an unsatisfying career is ruling my life right now, thank you very much." Okay, I realize that, but look beyond your immediate situation for a moment at the big picture that has led you to this point.

What rules your life? What keeps you up late at night? What motivates you and drives your decisions? C'mon, be honest with yourself. Don't give me a canned or politically correct answer. Why do you do what you do for a living . . . or at least what you used to do? Here are a few common answers. As you read each one, ask yourself, does it ring true for you?

> Until you make peace with who you are, you'll never be content with what you have.
> —*Doris Mortman*

Keeping Up with the Joneses, the Smiths, and Everybody Else

Is the pursuit of material things or the peer pressure to "keep up" ruling your life? In cities all over America you have what I call your 50-K millionaires. These folks are "all show and no dough." They drive the Lexus and live the million-dollar lifestyle but they make only $50,000 a year (a great salary for a huge part of the population, but not enough to support a luxury lifestyle). They are constantly looking around to see what other people have or are comparing themselves to their peers, friends, and neighbors. It is a race with no finish line.

Upon starting my career, I received one of the best pieces of advice from one of my early mentors, Bob Gordon, who said, "Whether someone is twenty-five or fifty-five, people always compare themselves to one another. No matter how successful you are, there will always be someone with more or who makes more money. Be happy with what you have." Wise words from a wise man.

We all size up the competition. Everyone has a tinge of jealousy or envy at some point, but the bottom line is whether or not your desire to keep up with others is adversely affecting the rest of your life or preventing you from enjoying what you do have.

> **Success is not measured by how you do compared to how somebody else does. Success is measured by how you do compared to what you could have done with what God gave you.**
>
> *—Anonymous*

Trying to Live Up to Everyone's Expectations but Your Own

Are you living someone else's life? Are you being ruled by a desire to prove something to yourself or to someone else, such as your parents or peers? Are you trying to live up to someone else's expectations or idea of what you should do or how you should live your life? There is a fine line between doing what is "right" and allowing guilt to rule your life. As Shakespeare once wrote, "To thine own self be true."

Slave to the Job

Do you leave the best part of yourself at the office? When you have to choose between your work and your personal life or family, do you automatically ask your family to adjust? We all make sacrifices for our work, and hopefully you are rewarded handsomely enough to make any sacrifices worth making. Only you can be the judge.

Employers love to toss around the term "work/life balance," but often the scales are tipped in favor of the company. A survey by national staffing firm Office Team found that 70 percent of people surveyed felt they had a serious problem with work/life balance. Over 55 percent of people surveyed said they would consider a job that paid less but allowed them to spend more time with their family. Forty percent of those surveyed thought their employer was insensitive to family needs. All in all, those surveyed rated work/life balance above all other factors, even pay.

It is a cliché, but accurate: "A job can't love you back." Do you spend most of your time on airplanes and away from home? Do you enjoy the work and are you challenged and invigorated, or are you chained by the fear of not knowing what else you can do or how you would make a change?

> I wish that I had known sooner that if you miss a child's play or performance or sporting event, you will have forgotten a year later the work emergency that caused you to miss it. But the child won't have forgotten that you weren't there.
>
> —*Laurel Cutler*

> "How can someone say that this layoff is not personal? It is extremely personal to me. I've sacrificed for this company because someone else thought it was important that I stay late, get this done, be on a plane, work weekends, miss soccer or recitals, have drinks with clients. Something else mattered to them. Now it is my turn to do what is important to me."   —Maddie L.

Money, Money, Money, Money

In business, they say "money is how you keep score." There is nothing inherently wrong with chasing bucks, but take a moment to ask why you are letting this pursuit rule your life. Is it to prove something to yourself or someone else? Is it to increase your sense of self-esteem, importance, stature, or security? Or is your driving force to earn money so that you can send your children to college, purchase a home for your family, or save for your retirement? You are pursuing money, but what is your motivation for wanting the money, and what will the money do for you?

> We are prone to judge success by the index of our salaries or the size of our automobiles rather than by the quality of our service and relationship to mankind.
>
> —Dr. Martin Luther King Jr.

Debt and the Constant Pursuit to "Catch Up"

Everyone has some sort of debt. After all, most people you know probably have a mortgage and a car payment and they are likely to have a credit card with a balance on it. Kids need braces, they go to college, and they get married. Life happens, and it costs money. I know the financial planners and experts abhor debt (and rightly so), but the fact is, it is a way of life.

HOWEVER . . . this is not the type of debt I'm talking about. If debt and financial worries rule your life, you certainly know it. There is no guesswork. I'm talking about having huge balances that will take years to reduce, always having to juggle funds or finding yourself stretched thin or running short, becoming a master of cash flow to make ends meet, always worrying whether or not you can afford something, or praying that an emergency doesn't come up. Debt and worrying about money don't just rule your life, they consume your life.

Being a Part of Something and Contributing

Being part of an organization, a community, or a group can be a powerful experience. It is good to contribute and be needed. You may find satisfaction, energy, and camaraderie from being part of a group of like-minded individuals with similar interests who are working toward a common goal. Many people I spoke with were more upset by the loss of their work relationships and the fact that they couldn't contribute than by the fact that they lost their jobs.

> "Nobody depends on me like they used to. And I'm not dependent on others like I used to be. There was satisfaction in having someone need you."
> —Charles H.

Challenge and Achievement

We have talked about the peril in placing undue importance on your work and letting it determine your identity. However, it is also true that loving your work, striving to be the best you can be, challenging yourself, pursuing success, having a drive to achieve, be the best, or win, having the chance to use your talents, learn, and challenge yourself or to simply grow and expand your mind or horizons—all these can be positive forces in your life and can serve as a good anchor.

Family, Friends, and Faith

It may be that what rules your life and shapes your choices is your family, your friends, your faith, or your community service. Perhaps these things are your anchors. If so, you have a powerful tool that will help in your comeback.

This is not a complete list at all. You may have to look further at your life to determine what consumes, rules, or merely guides you. But whether it is something listed above or something you find by exploring your life further, your goal is to determine to what you are giving your best and, more important, to ask, "Does this deserve the best I have to offer?"

For a child, love is spelled TIME.   —*Anonymous*

Is Your Life Consistent with Your Beliefs and Values?

Sometimes you can start out on a trip with a particular destination in mind, but you can take a detour and end up miles from where you intended to be. In many ways your career and your life can do the same thing. You can hold certain beliefs, goals, and values that you fully intend to use as a road map or guide, but somewhere along the way external factors and internal choices alter your path, pushing you farther from the life you intended to create. You still know your beliefs and continue to recite them as your mantra, but the important question that a career setback raises is "Are you walking your talk?"

If the things we believe are different than the things we do, there can be no true happiness. —*Dana Telford*

Are you being true to what you believe and claim is important to you? If you say that you want to slow down and create more balance in your life, why are you looking for positions that keep you on the road five days a week or cause you to be stressed out? If you say that you want to make more money so you can provide a better life and material things for your family, why do you refuse to look outside of your low-paying industry or remain unwilling to consider a change? If what matters to you is creativity, why do you pursue careers that keep you in a box or are guided by rigid limits? If what matters to you is being around other people, why do you choose to work from your home in a city where you know few people? Be honest with yourself and see if you are living what you believe.

Knowing What Matters Helps You Define What Your Next Move Will Be

If you don't know what matters to you yet, don't worry. The questions raised in this chapter may have to simmer for a while before the answers make it from your heart to the surface.

They don't always appear as a billboard or a sign from the heavens. They may take a while and come to you slowly over time. When you do realize what matters to you, it might appear as an "Aha" moment or it may be a constant twitch that you suddenly realize is telling you what you have been looking for.

Regardless of how it appears, when you discover the answer, it is a powerful thing, but one question will still remain: "What can I do with the information?" Think of this information as a compass. You now have a tool that can guide you and serve as a way to keep you headed in the right direction. If your career setback has presented a fork in the road, being armed with the knowledge of what matters to you can make that choice much easier for you. Knowing what matters is powerful because it helps you choose certain companies, cultures, and opportunities—and avoid others as you make your next move and look for a career that is truly satisfying to you.

CAREER COMEBACK FUNDAMENTALS
Finding Out What Matters to You

◇ This is a temporary situation. When you look over the course of your career, it will be a snapshot of one brief period in time.

◇ Count your blessings and look at what works in your life. If you look for the bad things, they are all that you will find.

◇ Make sure the things that rule your life deserve your attention.

◇ Make sure your life and choices are consistent with what matters to you.

Step 6

Find Your Next Move

When you come to a fork in the road, take it.
—Yogi Berra

What is your next move? The answer is up to you, and it depends on a variety of personal and external factors. You may be in a situation where your next move (at least in the short term) is one of survival, requiring a stopgap measure until you can get back on your feet. It may be a retrenching where you plan to jump back into a company, industry, or situation similar to what you've known before. Or you may choose to make a turn and go in a completely different direction by changing careers, pursuing an entrepreneurial venture, going back to school, or opting for a change that gives you more "life" in your work/life balance. Career moves following a setback usually fall into one of three categories. They can be categorized as moves intended to:

◇ Maintain continuity
◇ Assure survival
◇ Change direction or set a new course

Moves Intended to Maintain Continuity

Never underestimate the power and appeal of a regular pay-check and insurance benefits. To some people having a job is as natural and regular as breathing, so it is important for them to find another job, preferably in the same or a related field. If you enjoyed your job, loved the industry you worked in, and want to remain in it, then your next move may be a very simple one. This can be a safe choice, since you know the industry and likely have experience and contacts. Here are the basic options should you choose continuity in your career.

Stay in the Same Industry, but Work for a Competitor

Contact your former competitors and let them know that you are on the market. To them, you are an attractive commodity. You have experience and contacts and you know how things work in the industry. You can hit the ground running, and you have knowledge of how one of their competitors works. You can bring insight and knowledge of best practices into the organization.

If you want to stay in the field, contacting your former employer's competitors should be one of your first steps. And don't mess around with the human resources department or look for openings on the Web. Start by contacting the head of the department you wish to work in, and let him or her immediately know of your experience.

Strange as it may seem, your setback may even be a blessing for you. In some cases, you stand a better chance of increasing your salary or obtaining a promotion by changing employers than by remaining with the same company.

Work for a Company That Serves Your Industry or Is Ancillary to It

If you love the industry you have worked in but want a different type of position, consider working for a company that services, is serviced by, or is otherwise related to your field. Your industry experience and transferable skills are attractive to an employer in the same or a related profession because you only have to learn a small piece of the business, rather than starting as a rookie. For example, if someone is in the advertising business and has had experience in television production and made commercials, her next move might be to work for a production house or at a television show. She could also go in a completely different direction and work on the client side, helping companies to work with advertising agencies.

Go Back to an Old Job

If you are still on good terms with a former employer, contact him to let him know of your situation, and tell him that you would like to talk about coming back. This may be your fastest way to land another job. You may have to swallow your pride or check your ego at the door. But don't think of it as a step back or an admission of defeat.

Depending on what has occurred since your departure, you might return in your former position or you may be able to come back in a more senior role. It is very unlikely you would come in at a lower position than the one you left.

You are incredibly attractive to a former employer because you know the job, the industry, and the culture and can hit the ground running. You may have been given a promotion at your new job, or gained additional experience, training, or skills, and are now worth considerably more than you were during your previous tour of duty. You bring more to the table because you have spent time away from the original organization and can offer a different perspective.

In addition to contacting your previous employers, call anyone who has previously offered you a job or who has expressed interest in you. Assuming that you declined the offer with grace and left the door open, there may be an opportunity for you. After all, if they were interested once, they might be again.

Slow Down by Going with a Smaller Company

You might have the skills and credentials to climb the ladder, but are tired of the pressure, the wear and tear, and the fast pace. You may be burned out and think that your work/life balance scale needs to be recalibrated. If you enjoy what you do but would like to slow down, consider working for a smaller company in your chosen field. If you have been a high flyer with a large organization, you are an attractive catch to a small-to midsized company (or nonprofit) that can use your experience and can offer a different culture that you might find more appealing. Downshifting to a smaller company does not make you any less attractive in the event it does not work out. Having small-company experience combined with tenure at a large firm can make you even more attractive in the long run.

Moves Intended for Survival

Sometimes you don't have the luxury of waiting for the "right" opportunity. Perhaps your industry (or bank account) has been decimated. Globally, hundreds of thousands of employees in the telecommunications, technology, and airline industries (to name a few) face diminished prospects and an industry or employment landscape that has been changed forever. If you are in this category (or if your search is starting to be measured in months or years), looking to work for a competitor or making a related change isn't an option. Your priority is just to survive and get by. If your needs are immediate, here are a few options for making survival your next move.

Freelance or Obtain Contract Work
with Companies in Your Field

Companies of all sizes frequently outsource projects or contract people to perform certain work. Employers love this because they can have a skilled person performing work, without the liability of a full-time employee and the accompanying cost of providing benefits. Freelancing or accepting a contract position allows you to earn an income doing what you are trained to do while you keep your skills up to date and sharp, and make additional contacts. It also gives you the freedom to pursue other opportunities should they arise. The downside is that you have no job security and no benefits, but it is a solid way to survive by working in your field.

Get a Part-time Job to Pay the Bills

Take a job, any part-time job that you can find to simply pay the bills. It can be anything—it doesn't matter if it is in your field or not. Just get something that gets you out of the house, around other people, and generating an income and contributing.

Some career experts may disagree with me about this, and you may have some concerns as well. Remember, this strategy is designed as a survival move, not as long-term career planning. If you have a financial cushion, plenty of options, and can wait things out and be selective, then this is not for you. Here are a few of the common concerns that people considering this move have:

"It is embarrassing and will hurt my self-esteem."

You're right. It may be embarrassing, but which is more embarrassing? Working at a job (no matter how overqualified you are) but contributing, earning your way, and taking care of yourself and others—or failing to do anything proactive to earn your keep or take care of your responsibilities, as you wait for something that "suits you" to come along? There is never any shame in doing the right thing, being independent, and working hard. I'm not asking you to do something demeaning but to put your ego in storage and do what needs to be done.

"It will take effort away from my main job search
and hinder my prospects."

Note that I said to get a part-time job. In fact I suggest a job totally unrelated to your field that is almost disposable (for lack of a better term). If an important interview or job opportunity poses a serious conflict, you can reschedule your part-time gig or (worst-case scenario) walk away from it—but always responsibly and on good terms. Never just fail to show up one day.

"How will it look on my résumé?"

It will never be on your résumé. You are doing this for some extra cash while you are in a bind, not as a career move. There is no need to put it on a résumé. If an employer asks you to describe what you have been doing or to explain a gap, explain honestly that you have obligations and have been working part-time to earn money to meet your responsibilities as you pursue your next career move.

It is a difficult thing to say to someone, but people will respect your honesty. It has been widely documented that this recession and job market have forced former executives and information technology workers who made $80,000+ a year to take jobs making lattes at Starbucks or working at Home Depot. It may be a far cry from where you planned on being (and it may be a temporary stop on your comeback), but no one worth his salt will judge you harshly for doing what is necessary to get by.

Work at Your Own Small Business While You Pursue Your Job Search

Use your hobby, sideline, or home-based business to generate some income as you conduct your main career comeback. I've known network engineers who have done landscape work, marketing executives who have sold homemade cookies and muffins, and analysts who have done odds jobs, handy work, and home repair. One person I know who collects and is knowledgeable about watches created a small storefront on eBay to sell and trade watches as a way to generate cash while he pursued his next career move. Look around you. A small business does not have to be a full-blown venture (as you will see below).

Moves That Take You in a Different Direction

So it is a brand-new day and you want to travel in a brand-new direction? Well, you are in luck, because there are options aplenty, depending on your stage of life, desires, and tolerance for risk and change. Here are a few of them.

Start a Company or Go into Business for Yourself

If you have had enough of working for someone else, then self-employment or becoming an entrepreneur may be a move you should consider. Being your own boss offers incredible freedom and financial opportunity, but beware of the siren song. Being your own boss isn't as easy as it may seem. In fact almost 70 percent of all new businesses fail within the first year. You can use the experience you gained from your former employer to start a similar business, you can pursue an idea that you have had tucked away for years, or you can buy into an existing business or franchise. There are many different types of businesses that you can start. Following are several ways that you can go about it.

Traditional Start-up

If you have an idea for a great product or service, then write a business plan and attempt to raise capital. It sounds simple, but getting a loan from a bank (for a new business) or seeking individual investors or venture funding can be extremely difficult.

These folks want to be paid back and usually only invest (or loan money) if it is a relatively sure thing where they are guaranteed a certain return or you have a mountain of collateral to guarantee the loan. Many start-ups and individuals can't provide that. You can use your own funds, assuming you have a nest egg, but you had better be confident in your plan or it is your cash that can go up in smoke.

Boot-strapping

If your plan does not require a lot of capital, then boot-strapping, or scraping by on a little bit of seed money while you use your revenues as a way to grow the business, is a great option. Starting small and building it up allows you to get your feet wet without risking everything. This is a popular option for people who consult or offer a service.

Franchise or Buy an Existing Business

Drive down any street or go into just about any suburban strip mall and you will find a franchised business. Many of the popular chains that we frequent, from restaurants to printers to cleaners, are franchises.

Franchises are popular in a down market or when unemployment is high. This is because many people who have been laid off are flush with cash from severance or early retirement and decide that they don't want to jump back into the rat race or that they want to be their own boss.

Franchises are a great opportunity because they allow you to become a business owner quickly by investing in an existing business or established business model and brand. Franchises usually require an initial investment as well as a percentage of all revenues. This is in exchange for ongoing use of the name, materials, supplies, marketing, and so forth. Depending on the franchise, the investment can be anywhere from $10,000 on the low end to well over $300,000. Financing assistance is often available. The one catch with many franchise opportunities is that it takes money to make money. Many franchisers conduct thorough financial background checks on potential franchisees and require them to meet minimum net worth standards, generally in the $150,000 to $250,000 range. If you got a nice early retirement or severance package or you have plenty of savings, franchising can be a great opportunity. To learn more about franchising, check out www.entrepreneur.com, www.startupjournal.com, or www.franchise.com.

One final thing to think about before you start a business. If you require (or enjoy) a regular salary, then do not go this route. Many entrepreneurs, at all levels, may go months without paying themselves as they attempt to get a business off the ground. Rather than pay themselves a salary, they invest money back into the business. In the beginning, starting your own business may have the feel of a full-time job, with all of the financial rewards of being unemployed. As for benefits and insurance, well, now that you are the big cheese, you get to pay for those on your own. Entrepreneurship offers big rewards but brings a big risk. Look before you leap.

In the end, it is important to remember that we cannot become what we need to be by remaining what we are.

—*Max DePree*

Go Back to School or Get Additional Training

Ah . . . graduate school, gateway to opportunity and safe harbor from the cold, cruel job market. "Should I go to graduate school or pursue additional education?" is one of the most frequently asked questions I receive. In a tight job market like this, returning to school can seem like an appealing option for "waiting it out" until the economy turns around or as a way to update your skills and make yourself more marketable. However, while knowledge is power, an advanced degree is not always the ticket to greater job opportunities, increased salary, or career advancement.

Now, let me go on the record early as saying that I strongly support postgraduate education. In fact, I don't want to dissuade anyone from pursuing education for education's sake. You can never have too much education or be too smart. Learning should be encouraged and pursued throughout a person's life. In the coming years a college degree will be the minimum requirement for many jobs, and you will be at a significant disadvantage without one. So, if you lack a degree or certificate of any kind (high school, vocational, or college), then by all means you should pursue it. An education will benefit you personally and professionally.

If you can afford it, are passionate about it, and it makes sense for you, then by all means . . . learn, live, and be happy. But the fact is that many people who pursue an additional degree or return to school after a career setback do so for the wrong reasons and end up throwing unnecessary roadblocks in their career path.

Let's take a quick look at some things you should consider before pursuing graduate school or an additional degree.

Know Exactly Why You Are Going and What You Hope to Gain from It

Why do you want to go back to school? Is it for the passion of learning? Does the subject fascinate you? Do you want to make a career change? Do you enjoy school and the campus environment? Do you feel that it can increase your value and lead to a better job? Does your company or industry demand it?

There are a variety of reasons and circumstances that lead an individual to choose to attend grad school, each as personal and valid as the next. However, there is one circumstance under which a person should never go to grad school. *You should never go to grad school to "escape a bad job market."* Your time is too valuable and school costs far too much for you to hang out because you either (a) don't know what you want to do, or (b) can't find a job, or at least the job you want. That is a foolish and expensive way to "wait until the economy turns around" and can be counterproductive in the long run.

How can an additional degree be counterproductive? Simple. After earning an additional degree as you wait out the job market, you are certainly more educated and more valuable . . . but you are now also more expensive than you were before. Rather than adding value, you are effectively pricing yourself out of the market by making yourself more expensive to an employer. Depending on how that employer or company views the degree, he or she may or may not feel that your advanced degree is worth the additional cost when compared with someone without the advanced degree who possesses more practical experience. You have paid good money for your graduate degree; you expect it to increase your earning power so you can recoup your investment. And this does indeed happen in professions where an advanced degree is required or where a premium is placed on graduate education. Yet in many industries, a graduate degree is a "nice to have," not a "must have," and therefore employers aren't willing to pay for the likely pay increase you would expect to get over someone without it.

Weigh the "Opportunity Costs"

If you are a business student, you are already familiar with this term. It basically means that going to school will cost you far more than your tuition and living expenses, when you factor in the lost income from being unemployed. Here is how it works. Let's say that you were making $40,000 per year before you lost your job. By pursuing a full-time MBA you are taking yourself out of the workplace for two years, effectively reducing your income over those two years by $80,000. (Of course, being unemployed for two years takes you out of the workplace and reduces your income by $80,000 too.) In addition to your lost income during that period (opportunity), you have tuition, living, and other education-related expenses that can range anywhere from $40,000 to well over $100,000, depending on your school and the program you enter. This means that your opportunity costs in this scenario are anywhere between $120,000 and $180,000.

Ask yourself, "Will my income after graduation rise significantly enough to offset those costs or allow me to recoup my investment in a reasonable amount of time (generally four to six years)?" If you expect your income to rise only slightly over what you were earning prior to grad school, then you might seriously reconsider.

Does Your Industry, Company, or Profession Require It?

Earlier I mentioned the phrase " 'Nice to have' or 'must have.' " If your career will certainly hit a dead end without an advanced degree, meaning that you cannot advance beyond a certain level without it, then graduate school is a necessity. However, if a graduate degree might (I said "might") give you additional understanding of your field, plus pay and a competitive edge, but it is not required, then think very seriously and ask yourself the next question: "Which does my company or industry place a greater value on, experience or education?" There is no correct answer. Each company and profession is different. It is up to you to discover the answer and act accordingly.

Another way to see if graduate school is right for you is to look into part-time programs, executive study, or other ways to get your feet wet and decide if you are prepared to jump in all the way. The bottom line on grad school is this: if you are passionate about it, don't let anything stop you. But if you are looking at grad school as a career advancement tool, weigh your options carefully.

Move to Another City

Sometimes a change of scenery is what you need to jump-start a career comeback. If you don't like where you currently live

WHAT ABOUT LAW SCHOOL?

You should think long and hard about the type of degree you seek. A legal education offers phenomenal training, whether you choose to go into law or business. However, law school is not only incredibly competitive and expensive, it is generally a three-year program, which can increase your opportunity costs.

Much can happen in three years, including the fact that you can change your mind about whether you want to practice law or not. Law school applications have risen to record levels. More attorneys are graduating each year and competing for limited spots with firms. With a sizable financial investment, not to mention the time invested, many people who entered law school because it sounded good, they couldn't find a job, or they didn't know what they wanted to do now find themselves forced to pursue a career they really aren't passionate about. Consequently there are a lot of attorneys who wish they were doing something else. Think hard about the long-term effects of what you want to do.

or if you have only remained there because of your job, now is a great opportunity to relocate.

If you don't have any serious obligations or ties to the community, like family, kids in school, a strong support network, or friends, then moving is an easy decision now that a job is no longer holding you back. But here are a few things to consider before you "load up the truck and move to Beverly . . . Hills, that is."

Choose a Location Because You Love It, Not Because of the Job Market

Move somewhere because you love the location or because you have friends or family there. Don't move to a city just to follow an economic trend or because it is considered a "hot" area today. The appeal and viability of a community that is built around a few companies or an industry can grow sour overnight (Silicon Valley, Telecom Corridor) and then you are stuck. The ultimate litmus test is "Would I still choose to live in this city if I did not have a job?"

Do You Have Contacts or Support in the New Location, in Case Things Don't Work Out?

Being in a new and strange city can be exciting, but scary. If you have a problem or an emergency or simply need a familiar face to talk to, do you have someone nearby you can lean on? You may be fine, but what about your spouse or your family? If you are at work all day or traveling, how will your family feel not knowing anyone in a strange city?

Get a Job First—Move the Family Later

If you don't have a job and plan to relocate in hopes of finding another position in a different city, be smart and try to land a job *before* you uproot the entire clan. While it may be more difficult on you, consider commuting or spending a few days or even weeks in the city of your choice as you attempt to land something solid before the rest of your family joins you.

How Do I Learn of Opportunities in Other Cities?

There are several resources that can give you a head start on choosing whether or not to relocate to another city and help you with your job search. Start by contacting the local chamber of commerce. Tell them that you are considering relocating to the area and ask them to send you a packet that includes a listing of top employers in the region. This may be available on their website as well. While you are at it, ask them what the local business publication is. It may be something like the *Atlanta Business Journal*. Most midsized to large cities have them. You will find a listing of them at www.bizjournals.com. These are great resources because they cover all businesses, large and small, and can devote more attention to companies than the local paper might. The best thing about these publications, though, is that they often publish an annual "book of lists" or listing of top em-

Pursue a Whole New Career Path

If you have worked in a particular field or been with the same company for a while, it can be daunting to think about making a major career shift. What are your options? Many job seekers stall their comeback because they feel that their experience limits them to a certain industry or that their only option is to work for a competitor.

If you are willing to look beyond your immediate horizon, then you will find that there are plenty of options available to you. Courses, assessments, and guides can be valuable in helping you to discover what else you can do, but before you go

ployers in a variety of fields, including contact information. If you are clueless about an area, this is a great place to start. The books generally cost about twenty dollars, but are worth every penny if you are serious about moving to a particular area. Don't overlook the local paper though. Many business sections produce a similar listing of top employers that is available on their website or for a nominal fee.

The last resource I suggest that you explore is one of the larger real estate firms in town. When you call, ask to speak to someone who specializes in relocations. Explain that you are considering moving to the area and would like more information on the economic climate. Believe me, they will be more than eager to help you. (You are a prospective client.) They likely have tons of useful information and packets prepared. Other people have done much of the legwork for you—all you have to do is pick up the phone or send an e-mail and ask for help.

down that path, let's do a simple exercise that can show you a few options.

Think of your profession as a river. A river often has little streams and tributaries that break off and form new bodies of water. They can go off in a completely different direction, but they are still related to the main river. Your career is similar. Your main profession or experience is the river (or main body of water). However, there are other careers that, while different from your main job, are related to or call for skills and experience similar to yours. They are like "cousins"—from different families, but still related.

Start by asking yourself what other industries, companies,

or professions are cousins to yours. For example, did you work for an insurance company? Who else does business with insurance companies? What other fields use similar skills? Did you deal with people in a specific industry, or contacts at a certain level? If so, who else might value your contacts or experience? What companies supply your industry and might value your insight and connections in the field? Who did your company sell to or provide services to? Could a former client value your experience? What other fields would be a logical move for someone with your experience?

For example, someone working in retail could make the leap from one type of retail store to another. The difference from selling books to selling clothes or watches isn't really that great. By the same token, while selling in a retail environment you may have developed sales or management skills, gained merchandising experience, and have had profit and loss responsibility, all of which can be attractive for a sales management position.

Here is another great example that demonstrates this concept. Let's say that you are a teacher. What do teachers do? They educate. They present and speak in public. They create a curriculum and materials that enhance learning. They must encourage people with different learning styles. They must be able to handle administrative functions and deal with a structured and bureaucratic environment. These are just a few of the things they do.

Now that you know what a teacher's common tasks and skills are, what other professions also require those types of skills? For starters, many companies have entire departments devoted to training and professional development. The people in these areas are responsible for creating and presenting training courses and seminars for employees. These trainers are essentially teaching, except instead of teaching

> There are some jobs that are transferable regardless of the field you are in. Sales is one such profession. So are marketing, accounting, and public relations. There are many more. Think about it. Health care companies, insurance companies, newspapers, technology firms, and publishing companies all have accounting, sales, and marketing departments (even IT departments, for you techies). Try to identify what other industries hire people with your job title and go for it.

history or English to seventh-graders, they are teaching adults about communication, diversity, and leadership, or a particular product or service. See how it works? Corporate training and development is a natural link to teaching.

Let's take it in another direction. What other profession uses skills that are similar to a teacher's? Some companies sell a product or service that can be rather complex to use or understand. Customer service or sales support representatives often work with a client after a sale has been made to train the client in how to use the product. While these aren't "sales" people, they use their teaching and communication skills to educate people.

You can't be expected to know the ins and outs of each profession and how to plug in your experience to different industries. That is where a career counselor or coach can come in handy. But this is how you should start thinking about and viewing your next move. Look around you and discover your natural links.

> It is not because things are difficult that we do not dare. It is because we do not dare that they are difficult.
>
> —*Lucius Annaeus Seneca*

Testing, Assessments, and Coaches

"Links, smhinks. I don't know what I want to do or what I'm good at." If confusion has set in and you want to go in a completely different direction, but don't know what to do or where to turn, here are several options I suggest you explore.

Testing

There is a plethora of tests, surveys, quizzes, and assessments that can help you to determine your strengths, talents, innate abilities, and personality traits. These tests can give you insight into what tasks, environments, workplace cultures, and professions you might be well suited for.

These are not your back-of-a-magazine "Am I happy with my career?" quizzes. They are often in depth and are generally administered by a counselor, teacher, coach, or advisor who has been trained in giving and interpreting the tests.

They can serve a great purpose and be very helpful to some people. They can be remarkably on target, but they are like horoscopes. They can be interpreted many ways, and sometimes you see what you want to see. They may offer suggestions for a career path, but that is all they do. I completed one elaborate skills assessment that said I was well suited for sales, writing, and working in a fish hatchery. True story. (Well, two out of three ain't bad.) You may find the tests helpful in offering suggestions and options, or you may find them best used to confirm what you knew or suspected about yourself. That information can help guide your next move and aid in choosing the right job and work culture for you.

How do you learn about these tests? If you have been provided with outplacement services, talk with your counselor and ask if testing and assessment services are offered. They are usually included in the package. If not, then a smart

---

PERSONALITY TESTS These analyze your personality, work, and communication styles. They can help you determine if your personality will fit with other people and in specific workplace cultures.

◇ MBTI (Meyers Briggs Type Indicator): A list of MBTI providers can be found at www.aptcentral.org

◇ Keirsey Temperament Sorter: www.keirsey.com

INTEREST INVENTORIES These are pretty simple; they help you determine what you are interested in and like to do.

◇ Strong Interest Inventory: www.career-intelligence.com

◇ CISS Campbell Interest and Skill Survey: http://assessments.ncpearson.com/assessments/tests/ciss/htm

◇ www.self-directed-search.com

◇ www.careerkey.org

SKILLS INVENTORIES These identify your skills and help you to find which are transferable to other fields.

◇ www.lifeworktransitions.com

VALUES INVENTORIES These help you to determine your motivations.

◇ www.career-intelligence.com

move might be to call the local community college and ask for the career center or counseling department. Explain your situation. They often provide these services for an extremely nominal free. That is your best value. You can also contact a career coach or counselor. Many specialize in career choice and direction and are qualified to administer and interpret the tests. Just make sure before you invest time and/or money in a test that it is designed to help you with your specific inquiry.

There are hundreds of assessment tools available that can help you determine a variety of things about your skills, values, aptitudes, and attitudes. Some are free and available on the Web, others cost a small fee and must be administered by a counselor. The bottom line is that one test can't tell you everything you need to know. They can be a good guide, cause you to think about a new path, and help you to explore your options, or they may simply be a confirmation of what you already knew. Don't put your faith in one test or accept the results as "absolute."

> He who would learn to fly must first learn to walk and run and climb and dance; one cannot fly into flying.
>
> —*Friedrich Nietzsche*

What Is Outplacement?

"Outplacement" refers to career management services for displaced or laid-off employees. (If you are fired you rarely get these services.) These professional firms, sometimes known as transition services, contract with your former employer to provide you with a package of workshops, counseling, résumé assistance, research, and sometimes even a temporary place where you can conduct a job search.

Programs and services can range from group workshops and one-on-one coaching to use of phones, office resources, administrative staff, financial counseling or planning, help with preparation for interviews or salary negotiations, and even networking opportunities. Some have internal job boards or databases that are available to their clients.

Certain outplacement firms can help you explore your options and may offer testing or assessment tools. They can give you information and feedback on how you can take your existing skills and transfer them to another field, and can even offer advice and guidance on whether you should start your own company. They are often in touch with the markets and know many employers, so while their job is not to find you a job, they can steer you in the right direction.

If you choose to use outplacement services, schedule your initial meeting as soon as possible. They can help you get your comeback off to a quick start and help cushion any emotional or mental blows you may have taken.

People find the services valuable but also benefit from the community, the people, and the objective expert advice. An outplacement firm provides you with a supportive, action-oriented environment, a destination, and structure.

You usually have access to the services for a set period of time (several weeks to several months).

What If I Didn't Receive Outplacement?

Not everyone receives outplacement. It is not something you are automatically entitled to. In almost all cases your former employer is picking up the tab, and it isn't cheap. Services can range anywhere from a couple of thousand to over seven thousand dollars per person. While all types of workers can receive these services, they are most often provided to white-collar employees.

Generally your former employer will contract with an outplacement firm, and the services (should you choose to use them) are provided only by this company. Occasionally you might be given a stipend or set fee for "retraining" expenses, which you can use to select your own program. If this is the case, shop around. Ask what different firms provide. Talk to former clients.

There is a growing trend for some outplacement firms to provide their services for individuals who have been displaced but were not provided with outplacement or an allowance by their employer. These services can range from résumé and cover letter assistance to allowing you to attend the support groups and counseling. Call one of the local offices for details.

The best-known firms include:

Drake Beam Morin	www.dbm.com
Lee Hecht Harrison	www.lhh.com
Right Associates	www.right.com
Challenger, Grey &	www.challengergray
Christmas	.com
Manchester Associates	www.manchesterusa.com

These firms all have a national presence, with many local offices. Visit their websites for details. Other resources can be found at www.kennedyinfo.com, which produces an annual directory of these firms, and the Association of Career Management Consulting Firms International (www.aocfi.org).

Career Coaches and Counselors

Have you ever taken golf or tennis lessons? Have you worked out with a personal trainer or taken a cooking class? The point is that you sought the advice and expertise of a professional to help you learn something. You can do the same to help with your career comeback. At some point you may need the services of someone who can guide, train, and advise you in an honest and objective way.

There are coaches for every type of individual. They are not all alike in skill, area of interest, type of client they deal with, or demeanor. Choosing a career coach or counselor is similar to choosing a doctor or athletic trainer. You may have certain requirements. You aren't going to see a dermatologist about a stomachache. By the same token, if you want an athletic trainer who will push you hard, challenge you, and not let you ease up, then you don't want a trainer who allows you to control the pace or who socializes while you work out. Each person's needs are different. Find a coach or counselor who matches your needs *and* your personality.

Some work with executives, some specialize in career transition or in working with entrepreneurs. Some coaches are better at listening and helping you work through feelings and determine what you want to do with your life, while others are skilled at formulating a no-nonsense nuts-and-bolts job search plan. It is up to you to talk with the coach or counselor to ask his or her style, method, and area of expertise. If you need a nurturing type, look for that. If you need a drill sergeant, go for it. Just realize that not all coaches are alike.

How Do They Work?

You usually agree to work with a coach or counselor for a set period of time, often in hour or half-hour sessions in person or over the phone. You may have a one-time session, but it is most effective if you work with someone over sessions that can last anywhere from a few weeks to three months or more.

Depending on your coach's style, the sessions may follow a planned format and agenda or they may be looser, allowing you to work on what you feel is important at that time. It is not uncommon for you to have "homework" or "assignments" from one meeting to the next. You may set goals together as well. The best things about working with someone else over a period of time are that you can gain a different perspective and learn of options that you hadn't thought of, you get the insight of someone who is objective and removed from the situation and can "tell it like it is," and last you have someone who is detached and objective enough to discuss your strategies, fears, or concerns in a nonjudgmental environment.

What Does It Cost?

The cost varies according to the coach's or counselor's experience and the services offered. Generally you are looking at a rate that can be anywhere from $50 to $125 an hour. As with anything, you will find some higher, but not many lower than that, unless the services are offered through a school or a religious or civic organization.

It is also common for services to be priced and discounted as a package. For example, you might get a price break if you commit to four half-hour sessions or a six-week program where you get one hour per week. Many coaches will offer personal access via e-mail or telephone throughout the week as part of the package. You may also receive some tangible materials, such as booklets, a summary or analysis, even résumé and cover letter rewrites. These items may be included in the price or offered on their own.

I know that money may be tight, but remember that a coach or counselor's fees (along with any job search–related expenses) are tax deductible. And while counseling may be costly, it can also propel you to a new career and a new payday faster, so it is worth the investment.

How Can I Find One?

Academic Institutions: I've said it before: the best value going is your local hometown college, university, or community college. Often it's your tax dollars at work, especially if you have a metropolitan or county-sponsored community college that is funded by local tax dollars. The community colleges often offer their services to the community (hence the term) for little cost. I know of one that offers testing and counseling to county residents for as little as ten dollars, as long as they live in the county and can show a driver's license.

The larger schools or even your alma mater may be able to help, but they are often limited to helping current students and alumni of a certain age. Generally, the services offered by a larger school are of more use to a recent graduate or to younger alumni. However, it is worth contacting your alma mater's alumni relations department to ask if they offer any services.

Religious Organizations: Many religious organizations have community outreach programs that offer career counseling services for free or for an extremely nominal fee. If you attend a job support or networking group, ask the leader if he or she knows of any programs. As with the support groups that have a religious affiliation, don't worry about the denomination. There is often little evangelizing or doctrine involved.

Outplacement Firms: If you are participating in an outplacement program, you already have access to a counselor. If you would like to continue after the package paid for by your former employer has expired, you should ask if you can do so on your own or if they can recommend someone. Some outplacement firms offer counseling and additional services to individuals for a fee.

Listings of Coaches and Counselors on the Net: You can find directories and listings of coaches or career counselors on the Web at www.careercomeback.com or at one of the following credentialed organizations: Coach University (www.coachu.com) or National Board of Certified Counselors (www.nbcc.org).

You can also type "career coach" or "career counselor" in to Google or your favorite search engine.

What About Credentials?: Each state has specific rules governing career counseling. Almost anybody can call himself or herself a coach. Just to show you that anyone can hang up a shingle and say they are a career coach, a story in the *Wall Street Journal* profiled a woman named Nancy Morris, who, after being fired from an administrative position in a "quasi government agency" in Northern Ireland, enrolled in a three-month tele-class to become a "career coach." Doesn't exactly instill confidence, does it?

There are organizations that offer accreditation and can verify the skills and credibility of a certain advisor, including the National Board of Certified Counselors, Coach University, or the Career Development Association, but in the end it is up to you. Do you feel comfortable with the person's qualifications, skills, personality, and agenda for working with you? I recommend that your barometer should be accreditation by one of the leading and respected organizations for counseling or coaching OR a demonstrated track record in the recruitment, career development, or human resources field. These people have "been there and done that" and know what works and what doesn't.

If You Are on Your Own or Don't Want to Talk to Anyone

Okay, so you are a lone wolf, live in a remote area, or are totally tapped. Looks like determining your next move is entirely up to you. Here are a few things that can help you to narrow the field.

Look at Your Past Interests

What have you liked to do in the past? What are your hobbies or interests? What did you enjoy about your previous job? Is there anything that you have wanted to do or pursue, but you were held back or made a different choice? Can you return to it? Can you make money from it (at least enough to keep the lights on?) and will it make you happy?

Ask Your Friends and Family What They Think You Would Be Good At

Talk about cheap coaching and counseling! Your friends and the people around you know you pretty well. They see what you get excited about and what you are good at. Ask them, "What do you think that I'm good at?" "What do you notice about me or think I should pursue?" They may see things in you that you have totally overlooked or have ignored. They may see trends in your past, your personality, or your experiences and can steer you in the right direction or dissuade you from making a potentially costly mistake.

What Is Holding You Back?

Go confidently in the direction of your dreams. Live the life you have imagined. —*Henry David Thoreau*

What dreams and ambitions do you have resting on a shelf somewhere? What are your goals? Do you want to work in a different field? Do you want to make more money? Do you want to make a greater contribution through your work? Do you want to be your own boss or have more freedom? Do you want to just slow down and not feel so pressured all of the time? Great. What's stopping you?

Have you always liked teaching, training, or working with others? Do you like negotiating, selling, and presenting? Are you more mechanically inclined? Have you been in a career that allows you to do these things? If not, what is holding you back?

I'm not asking this to be flippant or a smart aleck. There may be very legitimate reasons why you do not pursue these possibilities. I'm not naive enough to simply say, "Pursue your dreams and the money will follow." (The money may follow, but Visa and the electric company and the mortgage company will likely arrive first and are looking for money too.) I'm simply asking you to consider the things that have held you back from pursuing a goal, dream, or career change. I'm also asking you to consider whether your reason for holding back is legitimate and rational or something irrational that should no longer have control over you. Now that you are without a position, the future is a clean sheet of paper on which you can write a new plan if you choose.

So I ask again, what is holding you back? Are you scared? Do you fear rejection or embarrassment? Are you concerned about what others will think and about their perception of you? We all do things and make choices because they are expected of us. It can be out of a sense of duty or guilt. "My parents wanted me to do this." "I've been in banking for twenty years. It is all I know." "It is how people know me." "I can't start over."

Write down all of the things that are holding you back from what you would truly like your next move to be. As you write each one down, ask yourself, "Is it rational?" (based on fact), and "Is it irrational?" (based on a subjective thought or opinion, or not grounded in fact). As you look at each reason for holding back, ask yourself, "Is this something I can change or control?" and "Am I willing to make the change happen?"

Wisdom is knowing what to do next, skill is knowing how to do it, and virtue is doing it. —*David Starr Jordon*

The answer to "What is my next move?" won't always come to you as a "eureka" moment where the light bulb turns on. Nor will it appear as a neon sign, a billboard, or a pop-up ad saying, "Hey you, here is an opportunity that you should pursue." It is more likely that it will come to you over time, but it requires you to act and take a step in a new direction. Don't get hung up on your previous baggage or feel that you have to wait until the stars and moon line up properly for you to make your move. Once you decide on a course, devise a plan for how to achieve it and take the first step.

CAREER COMEBACK FUNDAMENTALS
Finding Your Next Move

◇ Know whether your next move is intended to help you maintain continuity, survive and get by, or change direction or set a new course.

◇ Don't use education as a way to "hide from" or "wait out" a poor job market. Go back to school if you need the education, it is required for your field, or it will make you significantly more marketable.

◇ Consider careers that, while different from your main job, are related to it or use skills and experiences similar to yours. Look for the natural links.

◇ Testing and assessment are valuable for offering options and suggestions or confirming what you suspected about yourself. But they can be interpreted in many ways. Don't put your faith in one test or accept the results as absolute.

◇ Use of a career coach or counselor can be money and time well spent. Each has a different style, specialty, and manner. Think of it like choosing a doctor or a personal trainer. Know what you want to accomplish and what you expect from the relationship.

◇ Ask your friends and family what they feel you would be good at.

◇ Don't let irrational fears or thoughts hold you back from pursuing a new path.

Step 7

Find Your New Job

*Destiny is not a matter of chance, but a matter
of choice. It is not a thing to be waited for, it
is a thing to be achieved.*

—William Jennings Bryan

The best medicine for a setback (and the best revenge
for getting fired) is to find a better job. While finding
a new job may be an easy task for some of you, many of
you are doing this for the first time in years, or in a field that is
completely foreign to you. You may know some basics about
getting a job or what employers are looking for, but recruiting
has changed dramatically over the past few years. Technology,
combined with the volume of candidates and the amount of
information available, has dramatically changed the hiring
process. Some of the old rules still apply, but many people try
to attack the job market using methods and skills that are an-
tiquated at best. Watching them navigate today's job market is
like watching an old science fiction movie where the villagers
try to attack the aliens with a pitchfork—not very effective.

This step (finding your next job) is likely the reason you
picked up this book in the first place. An entire book could be
devoted to each of the many elements involved in finding a

job—résumés, interviewing, cover letters, working with a re-cruiter, searching the Web—but when you boil it down, every successful job search is made up of the following steps:

- ◇ Finding employers and opportunities
- ◇ Getting in the door
- ◇ Selling yourself
- ◇ Closing the deal

If only it were as easy as it sounds. Over the next few pages, I'll help you work through these four main elements of a job search. I'll also let you know which methods work and which ones don't, and help you learn how to deal with the setbacks and rejection you may face as you take this next step in your comeback.

Finding Employers and Opportunities

When you build a house, you need a variety of tools to do the job properly. You don't just pack a hammer in your toolbox and hope for the best. Yet when it comes to finding a job, people tend to rely on one or two methods rather than use every tool available to them. Some of the most common tools for finding employers and opportunities include:

- ◇ Existing fans, cheerleaders, and suitors
- ◇ Former employers or clients
- ◇ The want ads
- ◇ Websites, job boards, and Internet recruiting
- ◇ Career fairs
- ◇ Recruiters, headhunters, and search firms
- ◇ Personnel, staffing, and temporary agencies

◇ Networking, contacts, and referrals
◇ Contacting employers directly

Some of these tools are more effective than others. There is no one correct method that is guaranteed to work every time, for every person, and in every situation. The best strategy is to incorporate all of them into your job search. Finding a job is a lot like fishing. You can have skill, know the lake, know your lures, and have a strategy, but it still doesn't hurt to have several lines in the water and hope the fish are biting. Let's take a look at the different methods you should consider using.

Existing Fans, Cheerleaders, and Suitors

Before you start worrying about launching a full-scale job search, look for the low-hanging fruit. Is there anyone you have met who has said, "If you ever want to do something else let me know," or "I'd love to have you work for me," or "If you ever leave this company or need anything call me"? If so, and the company or position interests you, by all means call them. Remind them of your previous conversation. Explain what has happened, that you are now on the market and that you would like to talk.

This is also true for anyone who has previously offered you a job that you have turned down. You may have turned down the position simply because the timing wasn't right or you were at a different stage in your life. Assuming that the job is appealing, that you rejected the offer graciously, and that you stayed in touch, there is no reason why the person who made you the offer wouldn't take your call. It doesn't guarantee that he or she will bring you on board, but it is worth a call.

Has a client, a friend, or a peer at another company ever

said to you, "I'd really like to work with you someday"? If so, call them. Companies now recruit many of their employees through "employee referral" programs, whereby an employee can receive a sizable cash bonus (several hundred to several thousand dollars) for referring candidates who ultimately join the organization. (You get a job and your buddy gets cash.) Companies reason that if their own employees are hardworking, intelligent, and enthusiastic, maybe they know people with similar characteristics.

These people see the value in what you do and feel that you would be a great addition to their companies. They can also be your enthusiastic champions and cheerleaders and can help speed the process along.

Former Employers

Another possible slam dunk to consider is contacting a previous employer (if you enjoyed the job and left on good terms). This may be your fastest way to land another job. People leave jobs for a variety of reasons that aren't bad at all. Maybe you started a business that didn't work out, you decided to try another field and discovered that it wasn't for you, or the industry cratered.

Sometimes the door remains open to employees who did a good job, left amicably, and stayed in touch with their former employer. Call your old boss and let him or her know what happened and that you would like to talk about coming back. You might be surprised. Even if there isn't an opening available at that moment, former bosses can be valuable allies because they know your work style, can serve as references, and can suggest other people and companies you should contact.

If nothing else they might be able to help you with contract or part-time work until something permanent opens up.

But before you rush back to a former employer, ask yourself why you left in the first place. You might have changed, grown, and developed but the company may be stuck in first gear. Also, you may be asked to come back at your old salary—it may be all that is available. That's fine depending on your situation, but on the other hand, since you have left the company you may have received a promotion at your new job and gained additional experience, training, or skills. You might now be worth considerably more than you were during your previous tour of duty. You may also be an incredibly attractive job candidate because you know the job, the industry, and the culture and can hit the ground running. If so, you should make a case for increased compensation.

Why the Want Ads Leave You Wanting More

Even in this day and age the want ads still remain one of the first places people think of to look for jobs. It amazes me how many job seekers naively rely on the want ads, thinking that the few pages of jobs that appear every Sunday make up the known universe of employment.

Look at the employment section in any newspaper in the country and you will notice how small it has become. Some newspapers report that their recruitment or employment sections have shrunk by as much as half in the past two years.

Unfortunately, it appears to be a trend that may continue, as fewer and fewer employers consider newspaper want ads to be an effective place to find prospective employees. This economic downturn has altered the way many employers attempt to reach candidates, forcing some to question the expense of placing numerous ads in print when they can cheaply reach more people for a longer period of time using the Web or other means.

There is also a growing trend for employers to place ads promoting the company as a place to work. This "employer branding" is often used to create awareness of a company and is intended to steer the job seeker back to the company's website rather than promote a single position or opening.

What does this mean to you as a job seeker? Simply that you should consider the want ads as one of many tools in your search. They are worth a look each week, but don't be discouraged by the lack of volume or lack of positions directly related to your field. Some industries and positions, including entry level, lower level, service sector, health care, blue collar, and some sales positions, tend to appear in the newspaper want ads more than others, but don't overlook your industry's publications, trade and association magazines, or newsletters. They may also have employment sections or post recruitment ads that are targeted for your specific field.

A final word on the want ads. While you may find fewer positions in print, most media outlets have seen the light and have invested heavily in beefing up their online presence with companion sites. Sites like www.careerjournal.com (the *Wall Street Journal*) and www.nytimes.com (the *New York Times* Job Market) list jobs that can be found both in print and online. Some jobs are exclusively found online. For a good list of newspaper and media sites, visit www.careercomeback.com.

Websites, Job Boards, and Internet Recruiting

So where are employers turning to find candidates? The Internet. But before you automatically think that using the

Internet for your job search only means searching one of the major job boards like monster.com, hotjobs.com, or career-builder.com, think again.

While the job boards are where most people turn (and subsequently turn away from out of frustration), the Web is useful in several ways other than searching for open positions. But like the newspapers, the Web is only one tool in your comeback toolbox.

Here are the most common ways that job seekers can benefit from the Web:

◇ Search and apply for job openings.
◇ Post your résumé into a database that recruiters and employers can search.
◇ Research employers, news, and trends or obtain contact names.
◇ Communicate with a community and have a sense of belonging.
◇ Seek advice, coaching, counseling, or job search help.
◇ Read content and articles that can aid in your search.

All job boards are not created equal. You can't simply choose one and think you have covered your bases. In fact, some estimate that there are over 10,000 job-related sites on the Web (the Web's second-highest category, behind sex sites).

Essentially there are three kinds of job boards:

◇ Major job boards
◇ Niche or specialty boards
◇ Corporate or employer websites

Major Job Boards

The current Big Three include monster.com, hotjobs.com, and careerbuilder.com. Each has its pros and cons, but one thing is consistent: they are all about volume. They cater to the masses. That is their genius—and their weakness.

Each boasts monthly traffic well into the millions. They also house literally millions of résumés in their databases. Various studies have discussed the number of résumés on the Web, and while no concrete or definitive figures exist, it has been reported that there is one job offer for approximately every 1,500 résumés on the Web.

If you are overwhelmed by the number of positions (many of which don't seem to be a good fit for you or are multilevel marketing or work-at-home scams), imagine what employers are dealing with. As of this writing, over 17 million people visit career sites monthly, according to Neilson/Net ratings. This accounts for 13 percent of total traffic on the Web.

Most employers use one (if not several) of the major career sites, but at the same time they complain because of the volume of unqualified candidates who respond to any one posting. One job opening may yield thousands of applicants—yet only a handful of those candidates may meet the minimum qualifications. As a result, more employers are turning their attention to creating their own sites rather than dealing with major third-party vendors.

Employers complain about the major boards in the same fashion that people complain about Microsoft's dominance. They may not like dealing with them, or may see them as a necessary evil—but employers continue to use them.

Some employers post job openings on all of the sites, but others are loyal to only one or two that are the most effective for them. It is certainly worth your time to post your résumé to each of the sites and to visit them every few days to search for new positions (you can also create job agents to do much of the work for you), but don't spend hours on the sites searching as if they were the only source of opportunities.

To use the fishing analogy again, searching on the big job boards is like fishing at the most popular spot on a lake. It is crowded and everyone has a line in the water trying to entice the few fish that are available. But if you go off the beaten path and find a little inlet away from the masses, you have less competition and much better luck. In your job search, this means visiting the niche and specialty sites.

A Sampling of Major Job Boards and How They Differ

www.monster.com—The biggest in the world, Monster caters to all industries and experience levels. The company behind it is also one of the largest recruitment advertising agencies in the world, so many of its clients post positions on monster.com as well.

www.hotjobs.com—Considered the number-two player behind Monster, hotjobs is owned by Yahoo and is another favorite among the supersites used by employers.

www.careerbuilder.com—With a strength in local newspapers, careerbuilder's primary partners are the Tribune Company, Knight-Ridder, and Gannett (three of the largest newspaper publishers in the country). Better suited for lower-level jobs in a local market.

Niche and Specialty Sites

When you're finished checking out the major job boards, make sure to visit the niche or specialty sites. These are the smaller sites that are devoted to a particular profession, industry, job title, experience level, or location. Some of these sites are independent, but many are associated with a particular publication, organization, or professional or trade group. These might include www.careerjournal.com, the official executive recruitment site of the *Wall Street Journal*, which caters to senior managers and executives, or www.dice.com, one of the top places for technical and IT talent.

There are sites that cater to every specialty field you could imagine. If you are in real estate, there are sites just for residential brokers, commercial brokers, developers, or leasing agents. If you are a recent college graduate, there are sites like www.monstertrak.com and www.campuscareercenter.com that are devoted to entry-level jobs. If you are a senior executive in the financial industry, there are sites for you. You name it, there is likely a specialty site for it. You should also visit the official website of your professional association or trade organization, as well as the website for the major industry magazine or publication. They will often have links to other career resources for professionals in your field. You can visit www.careercomeback.com for a comprehensive list.

Track Your Surfing

At the beginning of your search, create a list of all the sites you visit and register with. Make sure to mark down your password for each. It is also helpful to keep track of when you visit them

CAREER SITE INSIGHT

If you want to get the skinny on which career sites are really worth your time, I suggest that you check out *CareerXroads* by Gerry Crispin and Mark Mahler (MMC Group). They are a couple of on-line recruiting experts who compile an annual survey of over 2,500 career and résumé sites on the Web. They offer great analysis and are sought after by many of the top companies for help in using the Web to attract job seekers like yourself, so they know their stuff. You can pick up their book or you can check out their site at www.careerxroads.com.

Another great resource for learning more about using the Web as one of your job search tools is www.weddles.com. Pete Weddle is one of the nation's top experts on Internet recruiting, and his site and books offer special insight that can help you. He also has a phenomenal page that can link you to almost every major trade and professional association in the country.

and update how each has performed for you. This will help you determine which ones yield the best results.

Create Job Agents

Most sites (large and small) allow you to create a job agent or profile that sends you a daily or weekly update of recently posted jobs that meet the criteria you tell it to search for. These are almost always free and extremely easy to set up. You can have several versions set up on each site using different criteria, and you can give each one a different headline. When you establish your agents or profiles, don't limit them by salary. Leave salary requirements blank. When you limit your agent (or any Web-based search) to include only jobs in a certain salary range, it will only pick up jobs that list salary. However, most employers don't list salary or compensation ranges in their postings, so you would miss a ton of jobs because they would never be picked up in the agent.

Corporate Websites

A corporate site is simply the "employment" or "career" section of a company's website (for example, www.microsoft. com/careers). There is a growing trend for companies, especially larger organizations, to rely on their own websites more than on outside boards. It has been estimated that over 450 of the Global 500 companies post available positions directly on their corporate website.

Many companies, especially larger ones, are beginning to require all candidates to register and apply directly on the company's official site. This allows them to reduce their recruiting costs and build an internal database of candidates to search from when an opening arises. (I'll tell you more in a second about how to increase your odds of being selected from the database.)

In addition to job openings, you will find information about the company and the hiring process, basic benefit or compensation information, a description of what it is like to work there, and information about the company's culture. Individual departments may also have information about career paths, job descriptions, and comments from employees. (Great stuff, but realize that much of it is their own propaganda, so it has a certain "happy" spin.)

Each company's site is different. Most employer sites (or at least the better ones) will have a way for you to apply online or add your résumé to their database. It might be time-consuming to go through the process, but it is well worth it if you are really interested in working for that company.

The Web has revolutionized job searching and done much to bridge the gap between employers and candidates. But at the same time, it has alienated many job seekers by removing the human element from candidate selection. A job seeker who may have previously been selected because the person re-

How to Increase Your Chances of Being Selected Online

The key to being selected is knowing how job openings are written. Here is an exercise to help you. The next time you visit the major and niche websites, search for all positions for your experience level, title, and field, only DO NOT LIMIT by geography. Don't worry if a job is 800 miles away from you. You want to see jobs anywhere in the country.

As you review the jobs, look at each description. You will start to see the same words and phrases over and over again. Write them down. This is the language of recruiters. These are the trigger words that a program is likely searching for. Recruiters often write job listings and job descriptions. By determining the common phrases and key words they use to write the postings, you can begin to incorporate them into your résumé, profile, and cover letter. Include them in your descriptions and you increase your odds of being selected.

viewing the résumé "read between the lines" or was interested by a particular item on the résumé now might not be selected at all. That is because a computer program or system (instead of a person) is searching the résumé database for key terms. If your résumé or profile includes those terms, then you are selected. If not . . . sorry.

This is extremely frustrating for people with limited experience or who are making broad job or industry changes. Establishing a connection or relationship with a real living, breathing human being is harder to do, but more critical than ever.

The Best Way to Use the Web Is Not Looking for Job Openings—It Is Looking for Information, Trends, and Contacts

While most people use the Web to look for job openings, its most effective use is to research employers and identify opportunities beneath the radar. Start by reading everything you can get your hands on. Read everything from online industry and trade publications to newspapers, regional publications, and news releases. This will help you to stay current and fresh in your field (always helpful in interviews) and allow you to get contact names so you can bypass the usual personnel department route.

What are you looking for? Trends, who is hiring, and new developments, and one of the most useful hidden treasures—the contact names. News stories or press releases often quote executives or employees. For example, if a company is expanding to a new market, an article might be written to say, "XYZ Company plans to launch the new program in July, says Joe Blow, Vice President of Marketing." If you are a marketing person, "Joe Blow" is your main man. You now have a contact at XYZ Company. You also have a legitimate and compelling reason to contact him. In your call or your note you can say, "I read your recent quote in *Fortune* magazine and I'd like to talk to you about your expansion plans."

Of course you don't know Joe Blow, but at least it is a start, other than the nameless, faceless black hole that "personnel" or "human resources" can be. (You may end up there, but at least this gives you a fighting chance.)

There are also plenty of sites that are great for providing company research and profiles, employer lists, and contact information. Local newspaper sites also offer top employer or industry lists that you can use to gain employer contacts. It may take some work. Some are free and others can be accessed for a nominal subscription fee, but they are often worth it.

Here are a few of the most popular sites devoted to employer research:

◇ www.hoovers.com
◇ www.vault.com
◇ www.wetfeet.com

Check Out the Rumor Sites and Discussion Boards

There are many sites devoted to letting people vent or post opinions about working for certain companies. Many of them bill themselves as places to get the straight scoop on what it is like to work for a certain company or in a specific field. They are worth a look, but make sure to look at the source and form your own opinion. Depending on the site, many of the comments may be from disgruntled or former employees or just plain lunatics who haven't done their homework. On the other hand, you can sometimes get some really good inside scoop into the culture, which can help you determine if a company is right for you.

Go Where the Recruiters
and Human Resources Professionals Go

You probably have no desire to become a recruiter, but if you want to get the attention of recruiters or find out what really pushes their buttons, you should start thinking like they do and reading what they read.

As you surf the Web visiting the various sites and sources dedicated to your field, you should make a swim through the discussion groups, websites, and newsletters devoted to the recruiting and human resources professions. This is where the recruiters go for information and advice on how to find candidates. They need you as badly as you need them.

Visiting these sites and boards will give you an idea of how they think, where they go to find people, what types of candidates they are looking for, their turn-ons and -offs, and even names and contact information. Don't get bogged down in the serious industry talk or practitioner stuff.

Read the message boards and subscribe to the newsletter and e-mail summaries. If a site or a board asks you to register, go ahead. But in no way do I suggest that you participate in the discussions!

I do, however, suggest that you wait in the wings, read, and learn. You will discover their lingo, their concerns, and who the players are. You may notice a conversation or query in which a recruiter asks where she can find someone with over ten years of sales experience in the beverage industry or what the best site is for locating radiology technicians. If that happens to be your specialty, then cut out the middleman and approach this person directly. You have saved the recruiter time and possibly made her some money along the way. Also look for recruiters or firms that have placed people in your industry or at your experience level or title.

A few of sites that recruiters frequently use include:

◇ www.recruiter.com
◇ www.recruiterlink.com
◇ www.hr.com
◇ www.huntscanlon.com
◇ www.airsdirectory.com
◇ www.erexchange.com

How to Work a Career Fair

The bottom line on most career fairs is that, other than learning some things and getting your information into a company's system, attending one is like jogging on a treadmill. You work out and get sweaty, but after thirty minutes you are still in the same place. As far as effectiveness goes on the "job search food chain," career fairs are near the bottom.

Career fairs are all about volume. They are the Wal-Mart of the career world, in that they have a huge selection of products under one roof (employers) and a huge number of customers (candidates) who have come to see the wares. However, while people actually make purchases at Wal-Mart, very few deals ever close right at a career fair.

Employers go to career fairs for exposure and to build a candidate pool or increase their résumé database. They get to

CAREER FAIRS THAT "PRESCREEN" CANDIDATES OR ARE "INVITATION ONLY"

The idea of "prescreening" is great in theory, but it is extremely difficult to pull off in practice. Only a few have been able to do it adequately. The idea of true prescreening runs counter to the way most career fairs are set up, in that they attract a large volume of candidates. In many cases, the "prescreening" is about as selective as your "prescreened" credit card offers. You may belong to a certain group, organization, or association or fit into a particular demographic, but beyond that it is not as selective as it seems.

In the case of "invitation-only" events, these too aren't as selective as you might believe. The group of those invited might be quite large and actually pulled from a demographic group or membership list, as with prescreening. But it is a lot like those reality dating shows where thirty girls are invited to vie for one guy's attention. And the guy isn't really that special. One exception to this might be if a single company or division of one organization is holding a small event on its own. But as far as those with multiple employers in attendance, how "selective" can they be?

talk with candidates and screen applicants, but finding a great candidate at a career fair is like finding a needle in a haystack. It can happen, but you have to really sort through a lot.

The problem isn't you or the employers, it's the system. Most career fairs aren't set up to offer an environment that is conducive to effective interaction. Relying heavily on a career fair is the equivalent of pinning your hopes of finding a spouse on trolling the crowded singles bars . . . around 1:00 A.M.

The fact is, people often leave a career fair more depressed than when they arrived. It is a draining rather than energizing experience, partly because you see firsthand how much competition there is. Anytime you have something that is advertised to the masses, you can expect the masses. The number of people all vying for a sliver of a recruiter's limited attention is deflating.

What should you expect from a career fair?

◇ To learn something basic about an employer
◇ To talk to a live human being (for about ninety seconds)
◇ To get your résumé into their system

Don't expect more than that. If you get more, such as a direct contact, a lead, an extended conversation, or a callback, then fantastic, you are a winner. But when you arrive and see

WHY DO THEY WANT MY RÉSUMÉ AT THE DOOR?

Career fair organizers know that there is no possible way an employer can see every candidate who attends, so they collect the résumés and either package them in a book or burn them onto a CD and offer it (or sell it) to the employer. Now the really big question is, do the employers really sit down and go through these huge collections? No.

Unless you place your résumé directly in the hands of a recruiter or register on their site, you have no guarantee that the company will get it or look at it.

the throngs of candidates, and I mean hundreds if not sometimes thousands, all with the same goal as you, it can be dis-
couraging unless you manage your expectations.

Have a Plan

Plan your attack long before you set foot in the career fair.
Start by learning which companies will be in attendance.
Contact the career fair sponsors to ask for a list of exhibitors.
They have this information several days before the event, and
often make it available to the public via the Web or in print.
Study the companies and mark your top prospects. If you
aren't sure what a company does, go online and look at their
website the night before. After you identify the companies that
you absolutely want to see, go through the list again and mark
companies that aren't your top prospects but sound interesting. Note the booth number and location of each company.
Most career fairs offer a map or layout of the room. Study the
layout ahead of time so you can work your way around the
room more effectively.

On the day of the career fair, come prepared with the list of
companies that you want to visit. But before you make a beeline
straight to their booths, take a moment to "walk" the fair. Walk
up and down each aisle and look at all of the booths before you
start talking to people. This will give you an idea of exactly
where specific employers are located, how many recruiters are
in attendance, and how many people are lined up waiting to
talk with them. Why is this important? Because career fairs are
often set up like the aisles of a grocery store, and the last thing
you want to do is to cluelessly wander the fair like you are trying
to find the Oreos. "Walking" the fair gives you an idea of the
layout and how you want to approach each booth. That way

I was recently at a career fair where 3,000 people had lined up by 2:00 P.M. The organizers had to turn people away, even though the event was supposed to last until 6:00 P.M. Staffers turned cars away as they pulled into the hotel parking lot. In desperation people then began driving by with their résumés hanging out the window, asking staffers to take the résumés in for them.

when you are ready to strike, you can do so with purpose and confidence.

The earlier in the day you can attend, the better. Be there when recruiters are fresh, alert, and attentive. As the day drags on, more and more people show up and everyone starts to sound and look the same to the recruiters. By the fourth or fifth hour of saying the same thing over and over again, recruiters begin to lose focus. They are human, after all. Another reason to go early is to beat the rush of candidates. I've seen some career fairs stop letting people in the door hours before it was scheduled to close, because they couldn't handle the crush of candidates.

Don't count on having a long, meaningful conversation with the recruiters. For recruiters, career fairs are about volume. If they find a diamond in the coal heap, that's great, but they want to see and be seen by as many people as possible. For that reason you should keep your initial pitch as brief as you can.

Before you get in line or step up to a booth, stand off to the side and grab someone who is just leaving. Ask her how it went. What are the recruiters looking for today? What questions did the recruiter ask? This insight will help you to prepare and give you an idea of how to approach the recruiter. If you know that the recruiters are representing an engineering division, but you want to go into marketing, then you can quickly steer the conversation so that you can get a marketing lead. You won't have much time when you speak to a recruiter, so use it wisely by watching your peers.

Don't follow the crowds. At every career fair there are certain companies that have candidates waiting in lines seven people deep. These are often the "brand name" employers that everyone has heard of. But don't make the common mistake of neglecting companies because you haven't heard of them before or they don't have a line of candidates swarming the booth. These employers might not be household names, but they may offer more lucrative opportunities than the companies everyone is lined up to talk to. You might also get more

---

A career fair is not a group activity. Employers are interested in hiring you, not a duo. So don't take a friend. This goes double for taking family members, triple for spouses. You may laugh, but I've spoken with recruiters who have had parents come with candidates to career fairs so they could speak on their thirty-five-year-old child's behalf. Repeat after me . . . Don't take a family member.

As a father of three little ones, I know how tough (and expensive) it is to coordinate child care. But anytime you meet with a potential employer, make every effort to leave the kids with a care provider, friend, or relative. Sometimes you have no other option, but it isn't fair to children to drag them to a crowded career fair. Not to mention that it prevents you from giving your full concentration to either the child or your job search. It is hard enough to talk with an employer without having your kid tugging at your sleeve asking for chips or whining, "When can we leave?"

attention from the recruiters at these companies because they don't have everyone vying for their time.

If you have attended a career fair in the past, you may have noticed that some of the companies there might have only a couple of openings, if any. So, why would a company attend a career fair if they don't have any positions available right then? The key phrase is "right then." They may not have an opening at that exact moment, but that can easily change in six weeks or six months. Companies want to be prepared by having a talent pool to choose from when the time comes. They might also be gathering résumés for a particular division or department that couldn't attend. In addition to screening candidates and collecting résumés, one of the primary goals is to promote the company as a great place to work. It can be a branding mission, pure and simple.

Working with Recruiters, Headhunters, and Search Firms

Whenever I talk with someone who is making a career comeback and he or she says, "I've got a headhunter working for me," I cringe. Not because recruiters, search firms, or "headhunters" are ineffective. To the contrary, they perform a wonderful service. The problem is that too many job seekers fail to understand what search firms do, how they work, and most important, who they work for. Here is a hint . . . it isn't you.

Let's get to the point. If you make less than $75,000 a year, are fresh out of school, or are just starting your career, headhunters, search firms, and recruiters generally want nothing to do with you. Don't take it personally. It isn't you. It is just very difficult for them to make money by placing people in these categories.

Recruiters are interested in placing established professionals at a certain salary level in positions. The hiring company
pays the headhunter a fee (most often a percentage of one
year's salary) to locate candidates for its positions. If you're established in your career, headhunters, search firms, and recruiters can be useful. But you need to understand a few basic
things about them.

There are two types of recruiters and search firms:

◇ Contingency search firms
◇ Retained search firms

Contingency Search Firms

Contingency firms accept an assignment from a company to
find an individual for a certain position. The hiring company
is the client. The recruiter's job is to then search using contacts, databases, or any means available to find a slate of candidates that the employer can interview and ultimately hire
from. The recruiter's fee is contingent (hence the term) upon
the firm hiring a candidate the recruiter has found. Bottom
line: if he doesn't fill the position, he doesn't get paid. Contingency firms are the most common type of search firm.

Retained Search Firms

Recruiters who are on retainer are contracted by a company
and paid a set fee to find a suitable candidate for a job opening. It works similarly to contingency recruiting with one notable exception—retained search firms get paid regardless of
whether or not the company hires the person the recruiter

recommends. These firms tend to deal with senior executives and often at higher salary levels than contingency recruiters.

Companies Pay—You Don't

Working with a recruiter should never cost you anything. The company always pays the search fee, which is traditionally anywhere from 15 to 30 percent of your first-year salary. This means that if you make $100,000, then the company pays the search firm a fee of $30,000. Some recruiters may make only a handful of placements per year. This is why they aren't interested in spending much time placing someone below a certain salary level. If someone promises to get you interviews or find you a job for a fee—run. It is perfectly fine to pay someone for counseling, assessment or coaching or to provide you with help on your résumé, cover letter, or strategy, but no one can guarantee you a job or an interview.

Recruiters Work for the Hiring Company— You Are Simply Inventory

Remember who a recruiter works for—the employer. A recruiter hopes to make a perfect match. It is in her best interest to find a qualified candidate for her client. A happy client means repeat business and referrals. But never forget that her goal is to please the client and fill the position. If you are that perfect match, fantastic. If not, "Sorry, next in line, please." She is on to the next candidate in her stable. If another position comes up that you are a fit for and you happen to be on the market at that time, great. But you are not her immediate concern. Successfully being placed by recruiters involves timing. It's all about having your name or information reach them at the exact moment when they have a need that matches your skill set.

Realize that it is a mutually beneficial relationship. Approach recruiters with an attitude that says, "We can help each other. I'm a valuable package that you can place with an employer (and collect your fee), and you have access to the employers that I need. Let's work together."

A great opening phrase to use is "I've been successfully employed in the (publishing) industry at a senior level for the past fifteen years. My company recently was (acquired/downsized) and I'm interested in talking with you to see how my background and experience might benefit your clients."

WHY DOES A COMPANY USE A SEARCH FIRM WHEN THERE ARE SO MANY OTHER WAYS TO FIND CANDIDATES?

A company may choose to use an outside recruiter when it has a very specific need or situation. It may be planning to remove a person and can't advertise the position. Maybe it's trying to pick off an employee of a competitor, so it wants to operate under the radar and distance itself from any potential legal problems. It may use a recruiter to do the legwork in finding a person with very specific credentials, experience, or background. A company might not want to wade through thousands of résumés, so it hires a recruiter to present several candidates who meet its needs.

How to Find a Recruiter

Check out *Kennedy's Directory of Executive Recruiters*. It is a red book that you can find at your local bookstore or by visiting www.kennedyinfo.com. Also check out www.recruiterlink.com and www.aesc.org (Association of Executive Search Consultants) to learn of recruiters in your area or specialty.

You should also ask people who work in your industry and any of your contacts who work in the human resources field who they use or recommend.

Play the Field, but Be Up Front and Open

Always contact more than one search firm. You have no exclusive agreement or commitment. It is in your best interest to have your information and name in the hands of as many people as possible. Chances are extremely slim that you will be put up for the same position by two separate recruiters. The only rule of thumb is that if a recruiter recommends you for a position, you do not attempt to contact the employer directly. This shuts the recruiter out of his fee, is not ethical, and is a guaranteed way to ensure that no recruiter at that firm will ever help you again. You also want to tell a recruiter if you have had conversations with a company prior to his contacting you. This prevents any potential conflicts between the recruiter and the hiring company.

Other Important Facts to Know About Working with Search Firms

◇ Recruiters specialize. Some work with marketing professionals. Others deal in finance. Some specialize in the health care industry or graphic arts. Contact three or four that specialize in your industry, field, or experience level.

◇ If contacted by a recruiter, always ask how he obtained your name or learned about you.

◇ Recruiters should always ask your permission before submitting your information to an employer.

◇ Don't be put off if a recruiter does not initially tell you who her client is or if she appears guarded. She is protecting her turf. It is normal.

◇ For a candidate, the size of the search firm doesn't matter. Recruiters who are one-person shops can be just as effective as the big firms. Just do your research and make sure that they are credible and ethical. Visit www.aesc.org for more information on checking out recruiters.

◇ Although they are commonly known as headhunters, they hate being called by this name.

Personnel, Staffing, and Temporary Agencies

Personnel and staffing agencies are traditionally thought of as providing temporary work or only filling short-term assignments. This remains true; however, many firms use temporary placements as a way to get a candidate in the door so they can ultimately convert him or her to a full-time hire. These "temporary to permanent" placements, as they are known, can generate significant fees just like placements by a traditional search firm.

Personnel firms were once thought of as offering only administrative jobs, but you can now find staffing firms that place accountants, attorneys, even CFOs (chief financial officers) in interim positions. Visit the National Association of Personnel Services (www.napsweb.org) or the American Staffing Association (www.staffingtoday.net) to learn more about and identify firms in your area.

This can be a good thing for you. Don't automatically dismiss a temporary assignment. Inquire if it is a "temp to perm" possibility. Think of a temp assignment as a test drive. Employers can check you out and you get to try them on for size while you get paid.

Networking, Contacts, and Referrals

Almost every career guru with a pulse extols the benefits of "networking." While no one has been able to verify it, various sources within the profession claim that over 70 percent of positions are found through some form of networking.

To learn more about networking and establishing relationships as part of your career comeback, revisit "Creating Your External Support System" (page 133).

Networking Is Simply Asking for a Referral

Every day we offer referrals in almost every aspect of our lives. We refer and recommend movies, books, and music to people we know. We refer and recommend restaurants, vendors, and service providers such as cleaners or doctors. Referrals even extend to relationships, where we play matchmaker with people who we believe may have common interests.

It is true in our everyday life, and it is true in our careers as well. *People do business with, buy goods, services, and products from, and hire people who they know, like, and trust and who come recommended.*

If you think that you will send your résumé to a company and because of your sterling credentials alone, you will be plucked from the ranks, you are kidding yourself big-time.

Networking is not about having connections that date back to Plymouth Rock. It is simply about meeting as many people as you possibly can and establishing contacts or referrals. Whether you realize it or not, everyone has connections or can easily start their own solid network.

Meeting someone through a referral or a contact is like a seal of approval. Employers are more comfortable doing business with or hiring someone who comes recommended by a trusted associate than they are dealing with Joe Blow off the street.

Everyone you meet is a potential contact. You may have a direct contact with a person, or an indirect one by way of an introduction or referral to a third party. Your friends, your parents, your spouse, your neighbors, your attorney, banker, accountant, doctor, or a bowling or golf buddy—all of these people know other people. Everyone is a potential contact because you don't know who they can put you in touch with.

Opportunities rarely fall into your lap unless people know

that you are looking for one. Networking does not happen automatically. You must take the initiative to make contacts. If you need an introduction or referral, ask for it. Don't worry whether you will offend someone by asking. If they mind, they will let you know that they don't feel comfortable, or they can't help you. That's okay. No big deal. You never know unless you ask.

Some people will treat you well and others will blow you off. Expect it, but don't let it bother you. Smart people will make an effort and treat you well, even though they don't know you or can't help you right then. They realize that you could be a potential client or customer, and if not now, maybe someday. You might have something great to offer, such as a hot idea, and may be a potential employee or partner in the future.

Just because someone gets you in a door or introduces you to someone doesn't mean that you will have smooth sailing. Often it is only an introduction. You then have to perform on your own merits. People will help you make contacts and get in doors, but what happens after that is up to you.

Contacting Employers Directly

Sometimes there is a certain company that you want to work for. You aren't interested in whether they have an opening or not; you want to create an opportunity and meet their needs.

If this is the case, don't wait for a job to be posted. Contact the head of the department or division that you want to work in. Do your homework, have a purpose, and know how you can bring value to the organization. The fact that you "think you would be a good fit" or "have always wanted to work here" doesn't mean squat. You have to bring something compelling to the table, like the solution to a problem, a way to save money, or entree into a potentially lucrative client relationship.

If you approach a company directly, your best strategy is to first visit its website and get your résumé and information in the system. Don't worry if there is an opening or not. You are doing this to save time and have a quick response when someone tries to deflect you by saying, "Go to our website and register." This way you already have registered, so that obstacle is already overcome. It also allows a potential employer to quickly access your information if he or she is intrigued.

Using your research (which you have likely obtained from news and corporate websites or publications), you can demonstrate that you have done your homework and attempt to create an opportunity for yourself by addressing a need that you have identified.

> **I am a great believer in luck, and I find that the harder I work, the luckier I become.** —*Thomas Jefferson*

Think of Yourself as President of Your Own Talent Agency

Oddly enough, finding a job doesn't start with your résumé. It starts with your mind-set. You need to approach this step not as a job seeker, but as a business owner, specifically the owner of your own talent agency. Your business has one client (yourself) and one goal: to place your client (you) in the right role (job). If you successfully sell your client, and place that client in the right job, then you will receive a handsome fee (namely a satisfying job and a salary).

The bottom line is that *finding a job is your job* (at least for the time being) and should be dealt with in a professional and businesslike manner. (I say "business," but I mean the mindset you would apply to any job, including such fields as teaching or the arts. If you plan on getting paid for a living, then you are in a business of some sort.)

Outside of writing your résumé (which I will address in a little bit), here are some things you should do immediately to "set up shop" or establish your "talent agency"—and increase your chances of getting hired.

Be Reachable

Now that you no longer have an office and the e-mail that goes with it, make sure that you have a consistent way for employers (and contacts) to reach you. Earlier I suggested that you acquire a generic e-mail address. I also suggest that you designate a specific phone to be the main number where you can be reached. Your cell phone is a good candidate for this because it is always with you and is good for snagging a quick interview. When opportunity calls, you don't want to miss it.

A cell phone also allows you to have a professional-sounding voice mail message that is separate from your home line. The last thing you want is for an employer to call your house and be subjected to "We Are Family" being sung on your answering machine. Nor do you want to risk your three-year-old answering the phone and telling a recruiter, "I can potty like a big boy" or having your mindless roommate who never writes messages down tell you, "Some guy called about an interview, but I forgot his name."

Also consider getting a P.O. box to use for all of your job-related information and correspondence. Use it as your main address on your résumé. The main reason for this is privacy. If you post your information on the Web, you can't guarantee that it will be kept private, or know who is seeing it.

While we are talking about privacy, never, ever put your social security number on your résumé or anywhere it can be displayed in public. And don't give it out freely. While some employers ask for it on a job application, most employers will not require it until you get an offer or they want to run a background check—which is usually pretty far along in the process.

Create a Job Log

How will you gauge your success—other than if you get a job? The best way is to keep track of the critical aspects of your search by documenting them. This means keeping a detailed record of the numbers and names of companies you contact, résumés and letters you submit, and interviews you receive, as well as progress reports. You should also keep a record of your contacts, who they referred you to, and how those conversations went, so you can appropriately track your network and give thanks where it is due.

In your log of the companies that you apply to, submit a résumé to, or otherwise contact, mark the way you learned about them. Was it through a contact or referral, or a posting on the Web? Did you read about the company and contact them directly? Track your progress as you get a response or subsequent interview. Write down if you even received a response. How you keep your log is up to you. It can be in a notebook, journal, Word document, or spreadsheet.

The most important reason that you should keep a "job log" is in case you are having problems. Looking at your efforts and progress can tell you if you are headed in the right direction or if you are way off track. It can help you unearth any trends and tell you if you are putting in enough effort. How many responses did you receive? How many interviews? Look at the stats but don't dwell on them. Look at them to see what is working and what isn't. Do it periodically to see if you notice a bad trend that needs to be corrected.

Create a Weekly Road Map

At the beginning of each week you should create a road map for the upcoming week. This will be your guide as you prepare to present yourself to employers. (Again, think of it as a business. This will be your short-term business plan.) It should include the weekly goals you have established for yourself. Be specific. You can add your own personal goals, but they should at the minimum include:

- ◇ How many calls you plan to make
- ◇ Which contacts you need to network with
- ◇ Which days you will search the boards or update or refresh your résumé
- ◇ What meetings you will attend

At the end of the week, compare this map with your job log. Did you stick to your plan? What worked? What do you need to change? Be brutally honest with yourself.

How Much Time Should You Spend on Your Job Search?

There is no right answer. Some people let it consume them and work harder than they did at their regular job. But after the two- or three-week burst of energy that many people have at the start of a search, the round-the-clock calling, Web surfing, and networking can start to become counterproductive.

Your job search is a twenty-four-hour, seven-day-a-week challenge, but it doesn't mean that you should be actively pursuing a job 24/7. It doesn't even mean that you should be doing it straight through for eight hours a day or until all hours of the night. Your comeback is a marathon, but your actual day-to-day activity should be a drag race that consists of short, intense bursts of positive energy.

You miss 100 percent of the shots you never take.

—*Wayne Gretzky*

Get in the Door

Once you have your system set up and a plan for conducting your search, here are a few things to remember when trying to get in the door directly with an employer.

Never Ask "Are you hiring?" or "Do you have any openings?"

These have to be the worst questions you could possibly ask. It is the fastest way for an employer to get rid of you because all she has to say is "No, we aren't hiring. Good-bye." These are closed-ended questions that can only be answered with a yes or no. If the answer is yes, you at least get a follow-up question. But if the answer is no, what can you say then, other than "Thank you very much"?

Crazy Methods Rarely Work

You may have heard corny stories of how people have done wacky and outlandish things to stand out from the crowd or gain an employer's attention. These include sending a fork with a résumé and a card that says, "I want this job so badly I can taste it." Or sending a shoe with a card that says, "Now that I have my foot in the door, I want to tell you about myself." Some people think that they are making a statement by using a brightly colored paper or graphics.

Here is the deal. I think these tricks are cute and can work in certain circumstances—if you're in an entry-level job or you are in the arts or a field where creativity is expected or accepted. However, once you pass twenty-six, cuteness gives way to creepiness.

You might gain an employer's attention, but it is not always the attention you want. Here is an example. One morning I met with the head of staffing for a Fortune 100 organization. She was concerned because they had just received over four thousand applications for an opening they posted the night before on their website.

This was an incredible number of applicants for a job that had not even been up twenty-four hours. Surely there was a glitch. After researching it, it was discovered that over three thousand of the applications were from one person. Again, thinking that this must have been a mistake in the system, the staffing director contacted the candidate and asked if he had

Southwest Airlines, consistently recognized as one of the best places to work in America, is known for its open and "crazy" culture. I've seen people who have sent résumés that have been printed on Wild Turkey whiskey bottles (a favorite drink of former CEO Herb Kelleher) and résumés that were literally six feet tall and in the shape of a heart (Southwest flies out of Love Field). These were incredible creative works and they gained attention. The staff has kept them, along with other creative samples, in a closet. But they didn't land the senders a job. The problem is that if you send a six-foot résumé or a bottle of liquor, it can't be scanned or logged.

submitted his résumé more than once. Beaming with pride the candidate said that yes, he was up all through the night applying for that job—three thousand times. When asked why he did this, he said, "I wanted to get your attention." He did all right. The staffing director said, "Thanks, but no thanks, and do not ever apply again."

A Résumé Can't Get You a Job

Job seekers, regardless of age or experience, place undue importance on résumés. The chances of an employer hiring you based solely on your résumé are about as good as the chances of winning the lotto. A résumé will not get you a job—it gets you in the door.

It is important that it be neat, clean, error free, logically laid out, and clearly communicate your experience and accomplishments, but its only purpose is to pique an employer's interest enough so that he or she wants to spend more time learning about you. Don't dwell on the document. It is important, but it can't close the deal.

Forget the aesthetics, and spend more effort communicating your experience and how well you have performed in your previous positions. Results are what push an employer's buttons, not big words, generic descriptions, and a really cool font. Give the recruiter enough information to entice him and make him interested in talking to you.

If you need help crafting your résumé, talk with an outplacement counselor, career coach, or community college career advisor, go to a job search or networking group, or hire a résumé-writing service. You can expect to pay anywhere from $75 to $200 for a professional to help you prepare a résumé. You may pay extra if you want help with a cover letter. Most of the major career websites have links to or partnerships with résumé-writing services. You can also visit www.careercomeback.com for samples.

Remember the following tips when preparing your résumé.

Content Is King and Results Matter

Employers value substance over style. Don't just tell an employer what you have done, tell her how well you have done it. Stress your tangible results instead of offering a generic job description.

Keep It Short and Sweet

Unless you are a Nobel Prize winner, you should never have a three-page résumé, no matter how wonderful you think you are or how much experience you have.

Object to Objectives

What is your objective? It is to get a job. An employer could care less that you are seeking a "challenging and interesting position where you can utilize your experience with a profitable company that values diversity and its employees." If it is not selling you, don't put it on your résumé. An employer is about to fork over several thousand dollars to hire you. She is thinking, "That's nice, but what are you going to do for me?"

HOW TO UPSET A RECRUITER

The *Seattle Post-Intelligencer* reports that of five thousand recruiters and hiring managers surveyed, 92 percent said they had been inundated by "irrelevant" responses to job postings. Further, 71 percent said that most of the résumés they receive fail to match the job description. (Bad, but not inexcusable.) But when 63 percent of job seekers "blast" unsolicited résumés without any thought, things are bad. And 34 percent of applicants don't follow the proper online or résumé submission instructions.

WHAT ABOUT RÉSUMÉ BLASTERS?

There are some services that promise to "blast" or shotgun your résumé to thousands of employers at once via fax or e-mail. These are totally useless. Rarely are they targeted. Recruiters view them as spam, so save your money and go for a rifle rather than a shotgun approach.

Never Send a Résumé by Itself

A sure-fire way to make sure your résumé is deleted or thrown in the trash is to send it by itself without a cover letter or statement. Create a brief (four-paragraph) letter that can be printed or e-mailed to accompany your résumé. It should start by stating how you learned of the person you are sending it to. Name drop. Mention an article you read or research you did. Just let the person know that you are not spamming her. And never send a statement or letter that begins with "Dear Hiring Manager." It might as well say, "Dear Trash Can, I'm way too lazy to find a real, living breathing person to contact, so I really don't want the job." Everyone wants to feel special and to be called by name.

Keep Your Resumé in a ".txt" Format That Can Easily Be Pasted into an E-mail

Fearing a virus, many employers will not open an attachment that is unsolicited or from someone they are not familiar with. Be prepared.

Why Can't I Get a Response?

One of the most common questions I'm asked by job seekers at all levels is "Why won't anyone respond to me or return my calls?" Let me start by saying that in the overwhelming majority of cases, it has absolutely nothing to do with you, your skills or abilities, or the quality of your résumé or information. I know it can be disappointing and seem like people are being downright rude when you don't at least get a return call, e-mail, or acknowledgment, but you can't take it personally or let it dent your confidence. It has nothing to do with you; it has to do with priorities.

When you were working, how many unsolicited sales calls would you take? Probably not many. How many times did you get an e-mail or résumé and automatically forward it to human resources, stick it in a file, or hit the delete key? How many times did you set up a meeting so another person could "learn more about your business" or conduct an "informational interview" unless a close friend, relative, or important business contact directly referred the person to you? Be honest. Hardly ever. And if you really did stop what you were doing and respond to everyone personally, then you are a far better human being than either myself or the rest of the general population.

The fact is, finding a job (selling yourself, getting your information in front of the decision makers, or networking) is your number one priority. But you don't even crack the top-ten list of priorities for an employer. And that has nothing to do with you.

For all intents and purposes, you are the equivalent of a salesperson trying to get a piece of his or her time. You had better have a pretty compelling argument or reason why an employer would want to take time out to meet with you. An employer is always thinking, "What is in this for me?" And sometimes you can simply fall through the cracks.

Let me give you an example. An excellent candidate named Jim contacts me to discuss opportunities with my company. I don't have an opening, but he has the right experience and great credentials. I might be able to use someone like him. I want to bring him in for an interview and plan to call him the next day to schedule it. Jim is at the top of my to-do list for tomorrow. When I arrive at the office the next morning, I plan to call Jim to schedule his interview, but before I can call him, I receive a call from my largest client, who has a problem that needs my immediate attention. I spend the whole morning sorting out this problem and taking care of the client. Suddenly it is lunchtime. I leave for an hour and plan to call Jim when I return.

When I get back to the office, I have a voice mail from an employee who has a crisis and needs my help. I spend a couple of hours with him. I haven't been able to call Jim yet, but he still seems like a great candidate that I want to talk to. I look at my watch and realize that I have to leave the office and head for the airport. I have a flight at five o'clock to Los Angeles, where I will be in meetings for the next couple of days.

The next two days I'm unable to call Jim from the road. Meanwhile poor Jim is still an awesome candidate and has done nothing to change my opinion of him. By the time I get back from Los Angeles, Jim has gone from being at the top of my to-do list to being stuck at the bottom of the fourth pile on my desk. Other things take priority.

It is entirely up to you to get yourself in the door, keep the ball rolling, and make others see you as a priority by showing them the value in meeting with you. The smart strategy would be for Jim to continue attempting to reach me via e-mail or voice mail at least once a week for about the next six weeks (or at least until I told him to stop stalking me). After about six to eight weeks, you need to start from scratch with another approach, get a different contact, or move on. However, the mistake that most people make in a situation like this is that they give up too easily, fearing that they are being obnoxious or that the employer isn't interested. What constitutes giving up too easily? Generally most people stop calling or give up after two or three times. As Winston Churchill said, "Never give up. Never give up. Never give up."

USE VOICE MAIL AND E-MAIL

Don't rely on one method of communication. Some people favor one form over another. A contact of mine, a senior executive at Blockbuster, will never return phone calls. It doesn't matter who you are, you are lucky to hear from him two weeks after you have called. But if you e-mail him, you can get a response in a matter of hours. Frustrated, I once asked him about this and he said, "I receive so many phone calls each day that if I were to stop for each one and respond to all of my voice mail, I would never get anything done. But I'm in front of my computer all day, so when I get an e-mail it is easier for me to respond immediately." His phone strategy is to check his voice mail every day, but return all nonurgent calls once a week. Everyone has a different style, so cover your bets and use all of the methods available to you.

PRINT—AN OLDIE BUT A GOODIE

Sometimes what is old can be new again. People are becoming so inundated with e-mails and electronic correspondence from job seekers that some have recently told me it is refreshing when they receive a printed letter or résumé in the mail. Oddly enough, so few people do it (and even fewer do it correctly) that it can make a real impression and stand out from the thousands of résumés and e-mails that clog an employer's in box. But this doesn't mean that you should rely only on paper. Use all of the tools at your disposal.

The Difference Between Assertive and Obnoxious

As Tom Petty sings, "The waiting is the hardest part." As you wait for a response, you wonder, "When should I follow up?" "Why haven't they called?" "Did they get my information?" "Have they already made a decision?" "How many times should I call before I give up?"

Many people sabotage their comeback waiting for an answer that may never come. They fail to act or make a call out of fear of "offending" someone or appearing desperate or pushy. On the other hand, some job seekers are so aggressive you would think that they are the reason there are stalking laws and restraining orders. Here are a few tips to help you walk the fine line between persistent and pesky:

- ◇ Limit your follow-ups to no more than once a week.
- ◇ If you haven't heard from someone by the time he said he would contact you, it is okay to call him.
- ◇ Give someone a chance to call you back.

◇ Don't take a lack of communication personally.

◇ Don't give up easily. Too many job seekers give up after leaving three messages. Bump it up to six and then try a different method.

◇ Don't assume people remember you when you call. Refresh their memory every time by putting yourself into context. "This is Bradley, we met last week about the sales position."

Fortune favors the audacious. *—Erasmus*

Sell Yourself

Once you are able to identify an opportunity and get in the door, your next task is to sell yourself. If you find the idea of selling distasteful, think of the words of Charles Schwab, who said, "We are all salesmen every day of our lives. We are selling our ideas, our plans, our enthusiasm to those with whom we come in contact."

Why Elevator Pitches Don't Work

Most career experts will tell you to create an "elevator pitch" or a "two-minute commercial" to describe yourself and what you would like to do. Consequently millions of job seekers spend time crafting their perfect pitch, on the off chance that they are stuck in an elevator with a hiring manager or have a chance meeting with a CEO who would actually let them drone on for two minutes before having an aneurysm. These orchestrated "elevator pitches" are too often wasted on other job seekers at networking and support groups.

The idea is good in theory, but here is where it falls short and what you can do to create a solution. For starters, the amount of time commonly suggested (two minutes) is completely unrealistic. In today's fast-paced environment, there is no way anyone will realistically give you two minutes to tell them about yourself. Show me the stranger who will give you his or her undivided attention for two minutes as you go off on a monologue, and I'll be willing to bet that person is deaf or a candidate for sainthood.

Get real. I believe it is smart to think of your personal description as a commercial, but two minutes is more like an infomercial, not a commercial. Break your description of yourself down to true commercial increments:

◇ 15 seconds
◇ 30 seconds
◇ 60 seconds

These are realistic amounts of time in which to convey enough information to be descriptive without losing someone's interest. Start with the smaller increment and if they are interested they will ask you follow-up questions, which will allow you to use your longer versions. In an interview situation you should have a full two-minute "extended dance mix" version that you can pull out when someone asks the dreaded "tell me about yourself" question.

Think of conversations you have at a cocktail party or at dinner with new friends. When you ask someone you have just met, "So what do you do for a living?" you don't expect a two-minute overview of his or her life story. You want a quick (fifteen-second) description. If you are curious you ask a follow-up question to get more detail. Apply the same strategy when telling your story to contacts or employers.

When creating your short descriptions, consider the following points:

◇ Have a clear and positive story to tell.
◇ Be comfortable in describing your past and present identity.
◇ Be able to quickly and clearly describe what sets you apart from the competition and what you want.

You Want to Win the Job, Not an Acting Award

The other problem with some "elevator pitches" is that there tends to be a flair for the dramatic. (You see this a lot at networking or support groups, where people go around the room giving their "commercial.") You would think that these people are frustrated thespians who never got the lead role, as they enthusiastically chant their qualifications with the can-do spirit and enthusiasm of a high school cheerleader.

"I'm Bill and I'm a dynamic, results-oriented marketing executive. I'm a proven leader and producer with over twenty years' experience and I'm looking to join your team." Kinda makes you want to do the splits and say, "Go, fight, win!"

These types of "pitches" are cheesy to the nth degree; they are the professional equivalent of personals ads and pickup lines. "Hi, I'm Ted and I'm a Libra who likes piña coladas and getting caught in the rain. I'm looking for that special company where I can share my experience in IT and my days from nine to five." Keep it real. Use adjectives only when necessary and have a conversational tone.

It Is an Interview, Not an Interrogation

In most cases, selling yourself is done in an interview situation. It is easy to confuse an interview with an interrogation. In fact, many people think of it as a one-sided dialogue where an employer asks probing questions as you thoughtfully and enthusiastically come up with perfect textbook answers (and it doesn't hurt if your socks match and you are having a good hair day).

An interview is a two-way conversation. Make no mistake; an employer is checking you out. But this is your opportunity to check him or her out as well.

Interviewing is really pretty simple if you think of it as a conversation where you are getting to know another person and determining if you want to pursue a relationship with that person. Think of it like dating. If you are on a date, you don't limit yourself to trying to impress the other person. You want to see if this is someone you want to spend more time with.

There Are No "Perfect" Answers

"So where do you want to be in five years?" "Tell me about yourself." "What is your greatest weakness?" There are books on the market that claim to give you the best answers to these and countless other canned interview questions. Don't waste your money. While some answers are better than others, there is not one perfect phrase you can utter that will make an employer open up his or her checkbook and hire you.

The best answer you can give is an honest one from the heart, in your own style, and using your normal vocabulary and tone. Don't pretend to be someone or something you are not or say what you think a recruiter wants to hear. Life is short and work takes up too much of it for you to try to impress someone by being anything but authentic.

Have Energy Throughout the Day and with Everyone You Meet

Anyone can be energized and enthusiastic (or just caffeinated) in a thirty-minute or hour-long interview. But it is when you interview with several people over the course of a day that it's easy to really drop the ball. Maintain your energy. The most important person you meet with might be the last one you see.

Your Story Is Fresh to Each Person You Meet With

You may be sick of saying the same thing about yourself and feel like you are repeating yourself over and over, but while you are familiar with your story, the person you are speaking with may be hearing it for the first time. As the day wears on, you may begin to leave out important details of your story because you feel that you have said that already (and you have, but not to this person). Keep it fresh and enthusiastic.

Ask the Same Question of Each Person You Meet in an Organization

A big mistake job seekers make is that they ask a question once. "What's wrong with that?" you might ask. Simple. If you ask a question once, you might get the answer, but you only get it from one source and one perspective.

Ask the same question of different people and you will be-

gin to get a full picture of the organization. A fresh-faced
rookie who has been with the company for only two years is
likely to have a very different answer from the jaded veteran
who has been with the company for fifteen years and has seen
it all and done it all.

Your task is to take the information, weigh the similarities
and the differences, and come to your own conclusions based
on the comments. We all view the world from our own per-
spectives, and this type of questioning is how you gain a true
picture of an organization.

There Is No Such Thing as "Overqualified"

After running my own business for almost eight years, having
been an entrepreneur was an obstacle I had to overcome when
making my career comeback. Many employers were concerned
that I might not be willing to be in a large organization, or comfortable in one. This is a common obstacle for entrepreneurs
looking to get back into the working world. Employers think,
"She is used to running the show, how will she work with another person calling the shots?" or "He is simply doing this until he gets his next idea and then he is out of here."

Whether it is an entrepreneur or an employee with many
years of experience, employers can have preconceived notions
about candidates who possess certain types of backgrounds,
such as a certain experience or salary level, and sometimes
about people of a certain age. It can be a difficult task overcoming these obstacles, largely because employers don't let
you know of their concerns or they hide behind phrases such
as "You are overqualified."

I talk with people every week who have lost out on an opportunity because they were "overqualified." Saying that you

are overqualified is a pure cop-out, and you shouldn't accept it. This is exactly like someone breaking up with you by saying, "It is not you, it's me" or "This hurts me more than it does you."

Saying a candidate is "overqualified" is a cover for something else. Think about it. Who would a reasonable employer want to hire: someone who is experienced, qualified, and competent or someone who is inexperienced?

So, what is the real story when you lose out on a position because you are "overqualified"? Your qualifications have nothing to do with it. It is a way to package the other concerns an employer has about you. Here is what he or she really means:

◇ You are too expensive and wouldn't even consider working for what we will likely offer you, so why should we invest any more time with each other?

◇ You are set in your ways, will come with previous baggage and bad habits, and won't do things our way, so we would rather hire someone we can shape and mold who will drink our Kool-Aid.

◇ You will be extraordinarily bored and leave in six months, and then I'll be in the same spot I'm in right now.

◇ You will be a "know-it-all pain in the butt" who intimidates the staff.

◇ You will be a "know-it-all pain in the butt" who knows more than the manager (who is intimidated and fearful that you will take his job, once you expose his incompetence).

◇ You may take this position, but the moment the market turns or you get an offer at your previous level or position you are out of here, so why go through that pain?

Address Any Potential Obstacles Head-On:
Your Best Defense Is a Good Offense

Your best defense in situations like this is to go on the offensive and address any potential concern or major liability early in the interview. Don't wait for someone to bring it up, as they may never talk about it with you.

If it is an obvious concern like age, level of experience, coming from a different field, or being an entrepreneur, don't worry that you will be raising a red flag or drawing attention to something that an employer hasn't mentioned. Believe me, if they haven't thought about it yet, they (or someone else) will before you are hired. At that point it will likely be too late for you to respond.

Anticipate the objection with a simple phrase such as "You may be concerned how I will handle working for someone else, since I've owned my own business for the past few years. But I can tell you that I'm happy to hand over the reins to someone else and focus on what I do best." Take control of the interview and the information. Present your story so as to nip any concerns in the bud.

What If I Was Laid Off?

As I've pointed out throughout this book, there is no shame in being laid off. It happens frequently, and to more people than you think. If a potential employer asks you about your former position, you don't have to go into great detail or make excuses. Simply describe clearly and directly what happened. "My company went through several rounds of layoffs" (was bought out/was sold/went out of business). Short, sweet, and to the point. Move on.

What If I Was Fired?

That is a different animal. Nobody wants to come right out in an interview and say, "I was fired." People are "terminated" for a variety of reasons, some of which really aren't as damaging as you might think. I'm all for honesty and frankness, but let's be real here. If an employer asks why you left your last position, you don't have to immediately throw yourself on your sword and say, "I was fired."

How you respond depends upon how you were let go. If it was because of your performance, or a political issue, or "housecleaning," that can be overcome much more easily than if it was for a disciplinary or ethical reason. Don't be evasive, don't make excuses, and don't dwell on it.

For example, you can simply say, "The company and I had different expectations about what constituted success," or "There was not a good cultural fit between myself and the organization." Leave it at that, but expect a follow-up question. You are being somewhat evasive but you are addressing the issue. If they want more detail they will probe. You always want to be honest, but this doesn't mean that you have to go into great agonizing detail about it.

However, if you are ever asked point-blank if you were terminated or fired, then by all means you should acknowledge it. You should never lie about this because it will backfire on you, maybe not right then but it will backfire. Here is how. A smart employer will call your references and perhaps call your former employer. In addition to asking when you worked there, she may ask if you are eligible to be rehired. Essentially this means, would the company hire you back again if given the chance, or are you no longer welcome? While legally a former employer cannot bad-mouth you, speak poorly of your performance, or go into great detail about your departure, he can say that you are not eligible to be rehired, which raises a major red flag. It is better to address things on your terms when confronted about them rather than try to "slip one by" and hope that no one finds out.

What If My Former Employer Is Saying Bad Things About Me?

Sometimes a former boss may cross the line and bad-mouth you to a potential employer, sabotaging your chances with a bad reference. Smart employers today are cautious about giving out too much information about former employees out of fear of legal action. Yet some persist in talking too much. If you are concerned that your former boss is spreading untruths, damaging your reputation, or jeopardizing your opportunities, you might consider using a service that will check references for you to determine what former employers and others are saying about you. For a nominal fee (generally between $50 to $100) services such as www.jobreferences.com will contact former employers on your behalf to learn what is being said and whether you have a legitimate action against your former boss.

What to Talk About in an Interview

What Questions Should I Ask?

Your first day at work is a little late to discover that things are not what you expected. I believe that anything is fair game and open for conversation, with two notable exceptions: money and perks. Other than that, you can ask anything you want. As long as you use common sense and are good-natured about it, nobody will think you're being too obnoxious.

Okay, When Can I Ask About Money?

When you get the offer. Anything earlier is premature. If an employer brings it up first, then it is fair game and you can talk about it.

What If I'm Asked About My Salary Requirements?

Say nothing. This is a case where the person who says a number first loses. You may be asked this early on, maybe in the first

SHOULD I SEND A SALARY HISTORY?

Some postings ask for you to send a salary history. Don't send it. This is a screaming red flag that they are screening people based on salary. If you are too low, they think you are either a bargain they can take advantage of or that you are too inexperienced. If you are too high, you will instantly be knocked out of the running because you are too expensive. Send your résumé, letter, and any other information. You want them to be impressed because you have the right experience and can bring value to the organization, not because you fall into the right price range. Sure, you may be eliminated right from the start, but this is not how you create value for yourself.

phone interview or screening. Don't fall for this trap. Answer their question with a question. That's right. When they ask what your requirements are or what type of income you expect, don't say anything. Flip it around and ask what they have budgeted for this position. Don't worry. This is how the game works.

Be prepared for them to do the same thing and respond with "It is competitive for the industry and varies according to experience." Don't give in yet. Your next question should then be "Good, so what do you have budgeted as competitive for someone with my background and experience?" You put it back in their court. This will likely go on for about two or three turns. DO NOT GIVE A SPECIFIC NUMBER.

Your hope is that the recruiter will bend first and mention a range. If it is in line with what you were thinking, acknowledge that you are closer to the higher end of the range but are in the same ballpark.

If you are backed into a corner and have to speak first, then you should also speak in ranges. Make sure that the range is realistic and based on your actual experience or research.

Sites like www.salary.com and www.careerjournal.com offer salary calculators that allow you to enter your title, industry, experience, and geographic location and will give you ranges for the field. You might also check with your professional association or trade magazine, which also tend to conduct compensation analyses. Armed with this info, you can confidently say to a recruiter, "Based on data for the industry, someone with my experience should expect something in the $75,000-plus range. Is this in line with what you have budgeted?"

Good Interviewing Means Good Listening

What you say is crucial, but being a good listener is just as important. Listening before you speak will actually help you to speak more intelligently because the other person leaves clues to what the employer is looking for and what they value. Early in an interview or discussion, ask, "Tell me about the type of person you are looking for" or "Describe the type of person who will be successful in this role." Then sit back and listen. As they are describing this person, take mental notes and compare what they are saying with your experience. They are giving you the answer. All you have to do is listen. Here are some other listening tips.

- ◇ Don't use a script in your head. Don't think too far ahead of the conversation or worry about what you will say next.
- ◇ Show interest. Be in the moment.
- ◇ Paraphrase. Repeat what someone said to make sure that you understand.

Employers Don't Want or Need All of the Details

I have a friend who is rather loquacious. He is the type of person who, if you ask him what time it is, will tell you the history of time-keeping and how a sundial works. He is very knowledgeable but gets bogged down in details that no one cares about.

Some job seekers do the same thing in an interview, especially after a setback. Employers are interested in the relevant facts. If they want more detail they will ask. You are selling them on yourself. This means presenting yourself in a positive light, not filling them in on all of the details and minutiae of your past.

BE ON TIME

This sounds simple, but this little thing can blow everything else. Tardiness for an interview or meeting causes someone to think, "If you can't show up on time for an interview, then (a) how are you possibly going to show up on time for a job? and (b) you can't be too terribly concerned about getting the job."

Sometimes it can't be helped. Traffic, weather, poor directions all can cause you to be late. If you are running late, use a cell phone or take the extra time to pull over and call to let them know. When you arrive, apologize. Don't act as if nothing happened. Give a quick apology. Don't give a lengthy excuse. Just "I was lost, I'm so sorry." And move on. Don't dwell on it or keep bringing it up because you are embarrassed.

◇ Don't get bogged down in buzzwords or in setting up a situation.

◇ Be positive when talking of your former employer. A recruiter doesn't know the story, but the benefit of the doubt generally goes to the employer. So avoid certain phrases like "We had a personality conflict." Translated, that means "I'm a pain in the ass." Take the high road.

◇ When your last employment situation ended badly, don't be evasive, but don't air dirty laundry either. Less is more.

Mastering the Behavioral Interview

There are many types of interviewing styles, methods, and questions. One of the current interviewing trends is the "behavioral interview." This is a type of interviewing where you are asked to give an example of how you have handled a certain situation or exhibited a certain quality in your past experience. You may also be asked how you might handle a hypothetical situation.

The questions are often based on specific themes. A sample question might be something like "Tell me about a time when you had to put together and lead a team." There is no right or wrong answer to these questions. Employers are trying to get a feel for how you think and would respond to a particular situation based on your past experience. A confident, well-thought-out answer is the best way to respond. Here is a good way to prepare. Choose about five to ten topics or themes. Some of the most common themes employers like to ask about include:

- ◇ Teamwork
- ◇ Leadership
- ◇ Conflict
- ◇ Persuasion
- ◇ Overcoming a challenge or failure
- ◇ Achieving success

Look back on your experience and think of times when you dealt with these issues. Remember them and practice describing them as compelling but brief stories.

Keep a mental inventory of these examples so when you are asked, "Tell me about a time when you have exhibited leadership" or "Give me an example of when you have overcome a failure," you have a repertoire that you can confidently choose from. This keeps you from having to scan your memory on the spot.

Pray as though everything depended upon God. Work as though everything depended upon you.

—*St. Augustine*

Close the Deal

Always Ask for a Time Frame for a Follow-up or Decision

Never let someone end an interview by saying, "We will call you when we have a decision" or "We will be in touch." Take charge. It is okay. You are not being obnoxious or too bold. You might say, "I understand that you are speaking with many people, but do you have an idea of when you might make a decision?" or "Tell me about your hiring process. How long does it take?"

This lets you know what to expect. If the company's process requires that a job must be posted for two weeks, then go to a committee, before a second round of interviews can begin, it may be four to six weeks at the earliest before a decision is made. By asking, at least you know what to expect.

Follow Up Quickly

Regardless of what the hiring company's process is, it is imperative that you take the time to follow up with an employer or contact shortly after meeting. This means less than forty-eight hours after an interview. It can be a letter, a voice mail, or an e-mail. The method doesn't matter as much as making sure that your name is back in front of an employer while you are still fresh on his mind.

Let Them Know That You Want the Job

If you know that you want the job, let the employer know. Don't assume she knows or let her guess. Be passionate about your desire and eagerness. As you follow up, continue to make your case for your value and why you would be the best person to hire. Use specific examples and well-thought-out reasoning.

If Given an Offer, Always Sleep on It

It may be your dream job. It may be the end of a drought. Regardless, do not accept an offer immediately. Think about it. Sleep on it. Talk it over with your family or other people important to you.

Don't Make a Deal Out of Desperation

Desperation can lead to compromise. Sometimes you have limited options and you have to do what you can to get by. But if you have some leeway, be careful to weigh decisions carefully before leaping into a position just because you are tired of looking for a job. Make sure that it meets your needs and the needs of those around you.

If You Don't Ask, You Don't Get

You don't always get what you deserve, but you get what you negotiate and ask for. If you do get an offer, now is the time to negotiate. You want to push and get what you deserve (and maybe a little extra). Pushing too hard can get things off on the wrong foot, so be reasonable in what you ask for, but make sure to ask.

Hitting the Wall and Dealing with Rejection

Sooner or later you will hit the wall or run out of gas. Most people do at some point in their comeback. The rejections of a job search, no matter how well it is executed, can sap your energy and cause moments of self-doubt. How do you keep your spirits up during your search?

Practice Pragmatic Optimism

Also called cautious optimism, this essentially means keeping a hopeful yet realistic view of events. During a job search or comeback it is easy to become overeager when you receive a positive sign or ray of hope. You can also go off the deep end when you receive bad news.

Try to keep your feelings on an even keel. Accept facts presented to you as they are. Don't start reading things into a situation, overanalyzing it, or getting ahead of yourself. Look at each piece of information for what it is.

Focus on the Things You Can Control, Not What You Can't

Don't dwell on what you don't have control over. You can't guarantee that an employer will call you back or respond to your e-mail. You can't control whether or not someone sees your résumé, whether there was a candidate with more experience, or if there was a sudden hiring freeze. You can't control if the person you were interviewing with suddenly left the company, if the vice president chose to hire a friend of his, or if the company decided to go with an internal candidate.

There are a lot of things that you can't control, so don't sweat it. Worry about the things that you have control over.

Put Some Structure in Your Day

Your job offered structure. You had a place to go and something to do every day. And whether you realized it or not, that routine offered security and built confidence because you knew that you could successfully navigate what each day held. For some people a lack of structure can be unsettling. Regain your confidence by establishing some normalcy in your life. Establish a new and positive routine and structure. Get up at the same time each day. Have a regular workout time. Schedule regular breakfast or lunch meetings. Establish a certain day of the week to perform specific activities (Web Search Wednesdays or Follow-up Friday). Keep regular standing social or networking appointments. Go to your Starbucks or grab breakfast out before you return home to make calls. Help your spouse prepare for the day or get the kids off to school. You will feel more productive if you establish a structure like you had before.

Get Dressed

It sounds simple, but your appearance goes a long way to establishing a professional routine and demonstrates to others that you are serious about looking for work. It shows that you still take pride in yourself and haven't thrown in the towel. It also helps your mental outlook and puts you in the right frame of mind to talk to people about a job.

I'm not talking about getting dressed in a suit and tie, but making calls or surfing the Web unshaven, in your underwear or pj's, and sporting a shocking mane of "bed hair" doesn't exactly give your family confidence that you are on top of your game. Your appearance sends a message to yourself and to the people around you.

Create Little Victories Every Day

A quick way to build your confidence is to find some small way to succeed every day. Think of it as a football game. When a team is behind or their game isn't working, what do they do? They change their strategy and instead of looking for the giant seventy-yard pass play for a touchdown, they go back to the fundamentals of running the ball for short yardage, completing short passes, and making first downs. They aren't focused on what lies ahead in the end zone. They are focused on every down. When they have enough successful consecutive downs and move the ball consistently, they look up and they are in the end zone. Finding success in something every day, regardless of what it is, will help you keep your head up and not let the little setbacks run you over.

Establish benchmarks, milestones, or events that signify a victory or positive step for you. Here are a few suggestions for "doable" projects:

- ◇ Reaching a certain number of contacts
- ◇ Making a specific number of calls
- ◇ Getting a positive response from a key contact (or getting any response)
- ◇ Obtaining a solid lead or referral
- ◇ Getting a phone interview

◇ Completing your résumé
◇ Learning of a new resource
◇ Coming up with a new phrase to position yourself or describe your experience

These are not earth-shattering, headline-making events, but they are the small things that get you closer to your goal.

What If All I Get Is Rejection?

While getting rejected can hardly be considered a victory, at least knowing where you stand is a positive step. It is disappointing to get a rejection letter or to learn that there are no openings, but at the same time, isn't it better to know that you can check that organization off your list and move on, rather than live in uncertainty? Sometimes the anxiety that comes from waiting and not knowing can be a greater drain than the rejection itself. Check them off your list and say, "Next!" You aren't interested in how many rejections you get, because it only takes one offer to make it all turn around.

Know When to Back Off and Recharge

When things aren't going your way, it becomes easy to let the negatives pile up on top of one another. If you are a Type A personality you may try to fight your way through it and charge ahead, but beating your head against the wall isn't really making progress. Instead take a break and back off for a day or two. If you have the luxury of time and financial reserves, then take a week or month to mentally step back and review what has worked and what isn't working for you. Develop a new plan of attack. But regardless, refresh your batteries and try to tackle the problem from a different angle.

> **Our greatest weakness lies in giving up. The most certain way to succeed is to always try just one more time.**
>
> —*Thomas Edison*

Leave Nothing in the Tank

Your success from nine to five is directly related to what you do the other sixteen hours of the day. It is the behind-the-scenes effort that gets you in the door and makes people want to hire you.

Are you willing to do what the other person isn't? Are you willing to go the extra step, do the extra research, make one more call, or send one more e-mail? At the end of the day, you should believe that you have done everything possible to aid your comeback, that you have worked your hardest, that you have prepared as best you can, and that you have left no stone unturned. You can't control many things, but you can control yourself and the effort you exert. You may not be able to find a job that day, but it certainly will not be because of lack of effort.

CAREER COMEBACK FUNDAMENTALS
Finding Your New Job

◇ Use all of the job search tools available to you. Don't rely on one over another.

◇ Existing relationships, referrals, networking, and contacting employers directly are the most effective ways to locate opportunities. Career fairs and want ads are the least effective.

◇ The best way to use the Web is to look for information, trends, and contacts, not job openings.

◇ Look at how job descriptions are written and try to work key terms into your information and descriptions. They are written by recruiters, and these words are triggers that they are looking for.

◇ A résumé is meant to get you in the door, not get you a job.

◇ Content is king when it comes to your résumé. Focus on substance over style.

◇ Employers don't care what you have done as much as they care how well you have done it. Stress results.

◇ Recruiters and search firms work for the hiring company, not you.

◇ Be persistent. Don't call more than once a week, but don't give up after three calls.

◇ It is an interview, not an interrogation. Feel free to ask questions.

Step 8

Find Your Stride and Get Back on Track

What doesn't kill us makes us stronger.
—Friedrich Nietzsche

Y ou can breathe a sigh of relief. You are almost at the finish line. But your career comeback doesn't end the moment you find a new job. It takes time before you feel confident and stable about your environment, abilities, and life again. There might even be a minor bump in the road or detour along the way before you feel that your life is back to normal.

Your final step is a transition. You will make a transition into a new organization, perhaps a new career, maybe a new way of life. Now that you have been knocked down and gone through these challenges in your comeback, you still have to work hard so that you don't find yourself back in the same place you were before your comeback began. Over time, you will establish patterns of success and use the hard-won lessons you have learned over the past few months. When you see the light at the end of the tunnel, consider the following tips as you adjust to your new job and come to the end of your comeback.

News Flash—"I'm Back in the Saddle Again"

You may have fallen off the face of the earth after your setback or banished yourself to a self-imposed exile. Regardless, now that you are back in the saddle, let other people know where you are and what you are doing. Do it soon after you become settled in your new job.

Make a call, send out an announcement, or send an e-mail with your new contact information. Make a special effort to let the people who helped you network, counseled you, or provided you with leads know where you are. If you obtained your new position through a contact, referral, or introduction, make sure that you do something special for that person. It doesn't have to be anything special or expensive, just a small token of your appreciation—a note, a bottle of wine, a gift certificate to a restaurant, even flowers can be a nice touch.

Strong bonds are forged in a crisis. You may have met many people during your comeback, and been able to develop a rapport and a strong connection with some of them. Those relationships may prove to be helpful professionally, and some may develop into solid friendships that you will cherish for years.

A comeback teaches us about our character and the character of others. Now that you have found your next gig and are moving on, don't lose sight of the people you relied on. Stay in touch and remember who was there for you.

I Have a Job. Why Do I Still Feel Shaky and Uncertain?

Having a job or setting out on a more satisfying career path is an enormous relief and a great weight off your shoulders. But time is the only thing that can make a comeback complete. Not a job, money, or a new title—only time.

Even after you have been working for a while, a feeling of uncertainty can remain. Michael, who had gone through two layoffs in eighteen months, says, "It is nerve-racking to jump through all of these hoops to get the job, and now that I have it, I feel pressure that everything is riding on this."

It is a common feeling, and it takes a while for it to go away. No one relishes the idea of making a second comeback soon after landing a job, so it is common to want to hold on to it for dear life. A job or a new career can be exciting and offer relief and security, but you aren't totally liberated until you feel that you are going to be there for a while or have a few victories in your new position.

You may have been through a traumatic setback. This is not something that you dismiss easily. As in the end of a relationship, you have moved on, but it takes a while for the pain to subside. You have been burned and you don't want to go through that again, so you remain guarded until trust is re-established in your new relationship. Only then do you feel comfortable and free again.

Know Who You Want to Become

My friend Phil is the eternal bachelor. He is a nice-looking attorney who has no problem dating. Once I asked him why he has never settled down and he said, "I'm not yet the person who the type of woman I want to marry would be attracted to." That really struck me. Phil knew who he was and where he was in his life, but more importantly he had a vision of what he needed to do to become the type of person who would attract a specific type of partner.

Great, but you aren't looking for a partner. You are looking to complete your career comeback. That's okay. Take that same logic and apply it to your career. Are you the type of professional, employee, entrepreneur, or executive you want to be? Are you the type of person who could attract the employers and opportunities you would like to attract? Why not? What is missing? What do you have to do to become that person? Write down the qualities of the type of employee, professional, or boss you want to be. You are a clean slate, with no previous baggage or preconceived notions following you. Now is a chance to reinvent yourself and start fresh. Think of these things as you begin your new career and try to become the person you have always wanted to become at work.

Don't Go on a Spending Spree—Get It in the Bank First

I don't want to sound like a fun hater or buzz-kill, but get back on your feet financially, replenish the coffers, and build a safety net before you go on a wild spending spree.

I know you may have been through a financial dry patch and everyone deserves a treat, now that it is raining pennies from heaven. But the smart move is to wait until the money is in the bank, you have established some stability, and you know consistently how much money will be coming in the door. Even after you start a job, it may be a month before you see a paycheck and six weeks or more before you know exactly how much your net income will be after deductions for taxes and benefits.

That being said, you should take a small portion and set it aside as a treat, slush, or reward fund. You and the people around you need a break or something special for your work and sacrifice. Just don't spend it before you get it.

You're the New Kid in Town

Regardless of how much experience you may have, you are the new kid, the outsider. In the beginning you have to walk a fine line. You have to achieve results and justify your hiring, so you want to make an impression early.

But at the same time, you have to make sure that you fit in with the culture, avoid upsetting anyone, and are careful not to encroach on someone's territory or squash their pet project. After a setback, your enthusiasm and desire to prove something to yourself and others can lead to a "bull in a china shop" mentality.

Tread lightly. You may legitimately believe that you have a better way of doing things or that the current method doesn't work or could be improved upon.

Be mindful that the organization likely existed and survived long before you came on board. You have to understand an organization before you change it. There may be business, technical, personal, or political reasons why the company does something a certain way.

By thinking of yourself as the organization's new messiah or "waterwalker," you can quickly alienate the people around you. And if that happens, good luck. Your job has just become infinitely more difficult because the people in place will prevent you from succeeding or fail to help. Listen and learn—then act.

ATTENTION BABY BOOMERS AND BIG COMPANY
REFUGEES—BEWARE OF THE MESSIAH COMPLEX

You are especially vulnerable to the "messiah complex." Keep in mind that some of the people you may be working with or working for don't remember or care about the good old days. In fact, since generational diversity has become more prevalent in the workplace, there is a good chance that some of the people you work with weren't even alive when you began your career. Avoid the "good old days syndrome." Be mindful of your references and stay away from "I've been doing this since the 1970s" or "I remember when we did something similar in the early '80s." The same thinking applies to dropping your former employer's name constantly. "Well, at my old company, we did it this way." The people at your new company (regardless of age or tenure) have more skins on the wall than you do at the moment. You have to earn your stripes . . . again.

Know How You Are Doing and Where You Stand in Your New Organization

Think back to your previous position. Did your departure catch you off guard or by surprise? Taking charge of your career means knowing where you stand at all times. This is critical in a new organization where you are trying to make your mark, get results, and interpret and fit in with the culture—especially if you are in a probationary period, which can commonly last up to six months.

Sadly, many organizations wait too long to let employees know how they are performing or where they can improve.

Some estimates say that up to 85 percent of small companies don't conduct regular performance appraisals, while larger organizations may limit them to an annual review.

For this reason, it is even more important that you take control and ask your managers, the people you report to, even coworkers that you respect or trust, "How am I doing?" Don't wait for management to tell you or for the scheduled six-month review. Every six weeks (at least for the first six months) you should take it upon yourself to ask for an informal appraisal of your performance. Ask your manager how she would grade you on a scale of one to ten on certain aspects of the job. Don't expect to get a ten, but if you aren't pleased ask why she wouldn't rank you higher or how you can improve in that area. Ask how others perceive you and who else you need to meet, learn from, or establish bonds with. Detect and correct any problems before they become major career obstacles.

Don't Forget What You Have Learned

Remember the "What I Learned from This" exercise in "Step 2: Find Out What Happened"? You wrote a list of the core lessons that you learned from your previous experience. Once you have settled into your new position, it would be smart to review that list so you aren't doomed to repeat your previous mistakes. As I told you, I keep my personal list of things I've learned during my career comeback taped to my desk to keep me headed in the right direction.

You have learned some hard-won lessons over the course of your comeback. Now that you have another job, it is easy to want to cast away the past and the memories of what has happened. Don't fall into this trap. You have worked too hard to slip back into old habits.

Avoid Buyer's Remorse

Sometime after you start your new position, you will be feeling good and beginning to make progress when you learn of an opportunity that you passed up, or something that you had considered but didn't pursue, or maybe hear of a friend or former coworker who landed a job that pays much more than yours.

Your current job is fine, but this discovery gives you buyer's remorse. It is just like buying a car. You like your automobile just fine, until you see the Mercedes your neighbor just bought. As hard as it is, don't dwell on it. Fight it. Think about your life and the choices that you made. You made the best decision you could, based on the circumstances and information you had available at the time.

I had a serious case of buyer's remorse about six months after joining the *Wall Street Journal*. It was a major speed bump in my career comeback. There was nothing wrong with my position or the company, but before I accepted the position, I passed up an opportunity to work on a new venture with one of my former mentors at a prestigious outplacement firm.

The job was great, the company unmatched, the money risky but potentially enormous. It was a tough decision, but I took a pass. After being an entrepreneur for eight years and running my own show, I was no stranger to risk, but I wanted a break from risk. More important, my family deserved a break from riding the roller coaster. My contact and I maintained a great relationship and we agreed that we hoped to work together someday, but the timing wasn't right.

About six months later, after I started at the *Wall Street Journal*, I spoke with my mentor. I knew that his firm had been wildly successful during that time and the risk would have paid off handsomely. He said he wished that I'd come on board.

Those words cut like a knife, and I kicked myself in the rear for weeks about that decision. But after I settled down, I came to realize that I had made the right decision at the right time. While the other position yielded a financial jackpot, stability was what I valued at the moment. The risk would have been too difficult to swallow at the time. That may change in the future, but at the time I made the right decision. Once you make your decision, make the best of it.

WHAT IF I REALLY MADE A BAD DECISION OR DON'T LIKE MY NEW JOB?

What if your decision to join this new company was a bad one? Unless you are absolutely miserable and would be better off without a job, stick it out, but continue to look for another opportunity.

Treat it as a consulting project. You know that you aren't going to be there long, but for now it is an assignment that is paying. But more important, you are more attractive to an employer when you have a job, so use it for what it is worth. You have everything already set up; simply continue your search.

If it doesn't work out or you leave less than three months after you start—forget about it, literally. If you are there less than ninety days, don't include it on your résumé. Don't mention it. It never existed. It was a false start. If you are ever asked, don't lie, but don't make more of it than it was. Simply continue your search. If you were already unemployed, an additional three-month gap is not that big a deal.

How Will I Know That My Comeback Is Complete?

Only you will know when you have hit your stride and your career comeback is complete. It isn't marked by a date on the calendar or a specific event. It comes slowly over time. It is different for everyone. For some it is a few weeks, for others many months. For me it took just under a year before I felt completely confident again and could put my past experiences into perspective and look objectively at what I'd learned.

It isn't necessarily as if there is a thunderclap or one day you simply know that you are back. That confidence may come after you reach a milestone or achieve a success. It may come after your life has regained some normalcy (or at least you are comfortable in your newly defined normalcy). But eventually you simply recognize that you aren't worried about anything, you are functioning, you are contributing, you are satisfied, and life is good again.

Remember I asked you in "Step 2: Find Out What Happened" to keep a copy of the letter you wrote to yourself describing how you felt and what you were going through? I'll bet you were wondering why I asked you to hang on to it. Here is why. About six months after you have settled into your next job or career, pull out that letter and read it. Think back to how you felt at that time. Review in your mind the challenges you faced and what you did to overcome them. Think of the lessons you have learned over the past few months, the skills you acquired, and the strength you found in yourself and in others.

As you read the letter, look at how far you have come from that day. How different is your life? How have things changed? Be proud; you are the reason for this change. You have done what it takes and met the challenges set before you. You are a survivor. It is at this moment that you realize the distance you have come.

If you recall, in the introduction I started by describing a leisurely drive interrupted by a crash that set your career comeback in motion. Let's fast-forward several months and replay that scenario as you are driving home on a beautiful sunny day. You don't have a care in the world. You're familiar with the road. In fact you have driven it so many times it is as if you are on autopilot. You roll the windows down. As the wind starts to blow through your hair, you pop in one of your favorite CDs, turn up the volume, and let your mind begin to wander. "I'd like to try that new restaurant I read about" . . . "Maybe we should take a cruise this summer" . . . "I need a haircut" . . . "I think the kids need some new shoes" . . . "Things are going pretty well at work" . . . "The yard is looking pretty good" . . . "Maybe we will try that Thai restaurant." As you pull into your driveway, it dawns on you—you are home and life is pretty good.

Congratulations. You have made it and you are stronger, smarter, and better for it. As someone who has been through it, I know that this has been a difficult process for you, but the rewards are great and will only continue.

We are at the end of our journey. I want to thank you for allowing me to be your guide. I'd love to hear about your career comeback. Feel free to write to me at Bradley@careercomeback.com and let me know what has worked for you. I hope that this book has helped inspire you, given you a plan, and helped you to believe in yourself again. If you are still on your way to picking yourself up, stay strong—your career comeback is not only possible, it is imminent. Good luck as you create the career and life you want and deserve.

—Bradley G. Richardson
Dallas, Texas

CAREER COMEBACK FUNDAMENTALS
Finding Your Stride and Getting Back on Track

◇ Announce to everyone where you have landed. Make a special effort to thank the people who counseled you, supported you, and offered referrals.

◇ Simply having a job does not mean that your career comeback is complete. A comeback takes time.

◇ It is common to feel uncertain and shaky until you know that your new move is solid.

◇ Work to achieve results quickly.

◇ Be mindful that you are the new kid in town and you must prove yourself to others.

◇ You have a clean slate and no baggage. Know the traits of the type of professional you want to become and work hard to become that person.

◇ Replenish the coffers. Wait before you go on a spending spree, but do a little something special for yourself and the people around you.

◇ Know how you are doing in the new organization. Ask for progress reports if none are given.

◇ Don't beat yourself up over missed opportunities.

CAREER COMEBACK RESOURCES

MAJOR JOB BOARDS

www.monster.com
www.hotjobs.com
www.careerbuilder.com

CAREER RESOURCES ON THE WEB

www.careerxroads.com
www.weddles.com
www.monstertrak.com
www.campuscareercenter.com
www.dice.com
www.careerjournal.com

COMPANY RESEARCH

www.hoovers.com
www.vault.com
www.wetfeet.com
www.corporateinformation.com

LOCAL BUSINESS PUBLICATIONS

www.bizjournals.com

SALARY INFORMATION
www.salary.com
www.careerjournal.com

OUTPLACEMENT FIRMS
Drake Beam Morin	www.dbm.com
Lee Hecht Harrison	www.lhh.com
Right Associates	www.right.com
Challenger, Gray & Christmas	www.challengergray.com
Manchester Associates	www.manchesterusa.com
Kennedy Information (produces an annual directory of outplacement and career management firms)	www.kennedyinfo.com
Association of Career Management Consulting Firms International	www.aocfi.org

WHERE RECRUITERS GO FOR INFORMATION
www.recruiter.com
www.recruiterlink.com
www.hr.com
www.huntscanlon.com
www.airsdirectory.com
www.erexchange.com

CAREER SUPPORT AND NETWORKING GROUPS
Exec-U-Net	www.execunet.com
Professionals in Transition	www.jobsearching.org
Netshare	www.netshare.com
40 Plus	www.40plus.org
Five-O-Clock Club	www.fiveoclockclub.com

Comprehensive listings of meetings and groups can be found at:

Career Comeback	www.careercomeback.com
CareerJournal	www.careerjournal.com
Riley Guide	www.rileyguide.com

ASSOCIATIONS AND ORGANIZATIONS

American Society of   www.asaenet.org
  Association Executives

REFERENCE CHECKING

www.jobreferences.com

FINANCIAL AND CREDIT INFORMATION

www.finishrich.com
www.bendover.com

FRANCHISE INFORMATION

www.startup.com
www.entrepreneur.com
www.franchise.com

SKILLS AND ASSESSMENT INFORMATION

www.aptcentral.org
www.keirsey.com
www.self-directed-search.com
www.careerkey.org
www.lifeworktransitions.com
www.career-intelligence.com

GREAT BOOKS TO CHECK OUT

    ◇ *What Should I Do with My Life?* by Po Bronson
    ◇ *Second Acts* by Stephen M. Pollan and Mark Levine

◇ *What Color Is Your Parachute?* by Richard Nelson Bolles

◇ *Smart Couples Finish Rich* and *Smart Women Finish Rich* by David Bach

◇ *Please Don't Just Do What I Tell You, Do What Needs to Be Done* by Bob Nelson

◇ *JobSmarts for TwentySomethings* by Bradley G. Richardson

◇ *1001 Ways to Show Initiative at Work* by Bob Nelson

◇ *The Power of Focus* by Jack Canfield, Mark Victor Hansen, and Les Hewitt

◇ Anything written by Harvey Mackay

◇ Anything written by Brian Tracy

HOW TO REACH
BRADLEY G. RICHARDSON

Thanks for buying this book and investing your time in reading it. I sincerely hope that your career comeback is successful.

I'd love to hear about your progress and what has worked for you in your career comeback. Feel free to send me your thoughts and comments and notes on your progress as you get back on your feet.

For more information on any of the following, please visit www.careercomeback.com.

◇ My Free Career Comeback™ Newsletter
◇ Career coaching
◇ Hiring Bradley to speak at your event or to your organization
◇ Career Comeback™ Tool Kits
◇ How to attend a Career Comeback™ Seminar & Workshop
◇ Outplacement/Transition & Career Development Services
◇ Audiotapes
◇ Videos

◇ Other books by Bradley G. Richardson, including *JobSmarts for TwentySomethings*

◇ How to become a Career Comeback™ Coach & Seminar Leader

Bradley G. Richardson
Career Comeback
P.O. Box 701420
Dallas, Texas 75370
1.800.562.7627
Bradley@careercomeback.com
www.careercomeback.com

More Career Comeback books and a column are in the works. I'd love for you to be a part of them. If you have a story, tip, quote, or question, or advice that you would like to share about saving your career and making a career comeback, let me know. I'd also love to hear your inspiring stories of how you have turned a situation around in your favor. Contact me at bradley@careercomeback.com.

INDEX

ABOUT THE AUTHOR

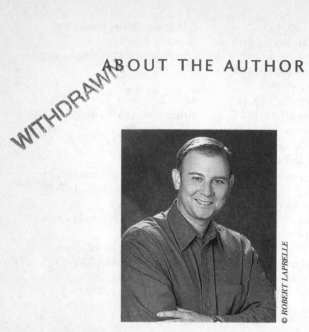

© ROBERT LAPRELLE

Bradley Richardson is the author of *JobSmarts for TwentySomethings* and *JobSmarts 50 Top Careers*. Richardson has spoken to thousands of job seekers and the companies that hire them at workshops, seminars, and conferences.

Dubbed by the *Chicago Tribune* "the perfect poster person for the downsized, restructured, shrink-wrapped job culture," Richardson has shared his JobSmarts on *Good Morning America*, ABC News, CNBC, Fox News, Bloomberg TV, and NPR.

Richardson is currently National Interactive Sales Manager for the *Wall Street Journal*'s official recruitment and career website, CareerJournal.com.